W9-AET-634

The Information War

The Information War

by
DALE MINOR

Hawthorn Books, Inc.   Publishers   New York

FOR ELIZABETH

THE INFORMATION WAR

Copyright © 1970 by Hawthorn Books, Inc. Copyright under International and Pan-American Copyright Conventions. All rights reserved, including the right to reproduce this book, or portions thereof, in any form, except for the inclusion of brief quotations in a review. All inquiries should be addressed to Hawthorn Books, Inc., 70 Fifth Avenue, New York, New York 10011. This book was manufactured in the United States of America and published simultaneously in Canada by Prentice-Hall of Canada, Ltd., 1870 Birchmont Road, Scarborough, Ontario. Library of Congress Catalog Card Number: 78–87868.

1 2 3 4 5 6 7 8 9 10

Contents

Introduction

"The Information War" is a phrase that came to be used during the war in Vietnam to describe the seldom physical but frequently bitter conflict between reporters and government officials working in that benighted country. The phrase is given wider application here, however, to cover a much broader and more profound conflict, that between the democratic imperative of full public disclosure and those forces and tendencies which act to constrict, control, and manipulate the information the public gets.

"The press" is ordinarily used to describe all or any part of the aggregate of newspapers, magazines, book publishers, and that portion of the broadcasting media devoted to the dissemination of news information, and so it will be used here. The term is frequently confused and used interchangeably with "the mass media." The usage is misleading, because only a portion of the mass media has anything to do with the gathering and reporting of the news, and in broadcasting, a relatively small portion. But if the press is quantitatively less than the media, it is qualitatively more than the sum of its organizations. It is, in a democratic society, the intelligence apparatus of those in whom ultimate authority is supposed to reside—the people. The institution of the free press in the United States is, next to the electoral process, the single most important instrument for maintaining that authority and, indeed, is prerequisite even to a healthy electoral process. It is the central nervous system of democracy.

The framers of the American Constitution may well have been idealists, but they were also inveterate skeptics. They operated on the thesis that power corrupts and that man has a strong propensity to be a rascal. The new nation, a revolutionary departure at the time, was structured on the essentially conservative thesis that while one might hope for the best, one had better expect the worst from men in government, and plan for it. And so, jealous of their own prerogatives and suspicious of the power they permitted others, the signers of the Constitution established a separation of powers among three independent branches of government—the executive, the legislative, and the judicial—and provided for a governmental process later known as the system of checks and balances. Their skepticism still unslaked, they decided, as an afterthought, that the people should be similarly protected from their government and that the individual should be protected in his rights from both the government and the majority of his fellow citizens. Three years after the Constitution was signed, the first ten amendments were tacked on to it—the Bill of Rights—providing for freedom of speech, worship, assembly; the right to petition the government; and freedom of press. Thus was the press established, in effect, as an independent institution beyond the normal controls of government and as an exterior check upon the three formal branches of government and their activities.

From that time to this the independence of the press has served as a kind of barometer of the political weather and the condition of democracy. Every major antidemocratic movement and piece of legislation in the nation's history has in some way attempted the control and/or suppression of the press and the restriction of press freedom guaranteed in the First Amendment. The Alien and Sedition Acts of 1798, the Espionage Acts of 1917, the Alien Registration Act of 1940—each either explicitly or implicitly infringed upon the freedom of the press. The Minnesota "gag" laws (ruled unconstitutional by the Supreme Court in 1931) and the Louisiana newspaper tax law (ruled unconstitutional in 1936) were deliberately aimed at constricting that freedom. During World War II Congress established the U.S. Office of Censorship, the first of its kind in the nation's history, consonant with what many felt was a necessary general restriction of the democratic process and of individual rights and liberties. In 1958 the government charged three American citizens with sedition (under the 1940 act) for publishing accusations in the *China Monthly Review,* a magazine published in Shanghai, that the United States had used germ warfare in the Korean conflict. The charge, in effect, was seditious *libel,* and proof that the "libel" was true might have been adequate defense. The defendants could not prove their accusations were true, but then the government could not absolutely prove they were false, and the charges were eventually dropped. The movement known as McCarthyism seriously endangered the freedom of the press—as it did freedom of speech, assembly, and petition—through a series of extralegal but not illegal techniques, principal among which was the institution of blacklisting, some of the effects of which are still felt today. And in 1969 a broad-gauged attack by the government on the forms of growing dissent, an attack marked by conspiracy trials and a heavy infiltration of dissident groups by government undercover agents, was escalated to include the press in a sudden but carefully orchestrated Administration campaign inaugurated by its cheerleader, Vice President Spiro T. Agnew, in a speech that denounced the television networks for, among other things, having dared to present critiques of President Richard M. Nixon's November 3, 1969, address on his Vietnam policy.

The old motto "And the truth shall make you free" has a critical political application. Although the truth may not, by itself, be quite sufficient to make or keep anyone free, the full and free flow of truthful information is clearly necessary to any kind of social and political freedom. And conversely, any serious attempt to abridge that freedom must include, and is often introduced by, an effort to direct or choke off the flow. To change metaphors, a burglar cannot operate easily or safely in a well-lit area, and a competent and independent press provides such light for the democratic process. It is this writer's belief that there has been a good deal of tampering with the electrical system in recent years.

To suggest that there is a serious and growing threat to the functioning of a free and independent press today is not to monger paranoid conspiracy theories. Indeed, were the problem the result of some malevolent conspiracy, it would be far easier to diagnose and much more amenable to corrective action. Instead, the threat to the function of the press and to the free flow of information comes from a number of independent (though not always completely unrelated) sources that have tended to complement and nourish one another and are now coalescing in what I feel to be a profound danger to American democracy. The ever-widening scope of governmental activities, the growing use of secrecy by government to control information at the source, the opportunity thus afforded government to manipulate the information the public receives, and the proclivity of government to exploit that opportunity are among the most powerful components of the threat.

The attitudes of the public itself are a significant and alarming part of the problem. "Newsmen everywhere—both TV superstars and reporters on the beat—are discovering an enormous outpouring of hostility. Significantly it ranges across the entire political spectrum." The quote is from a two-page "Press" story in the September 16, 1968, issue of *Newsweek,* taking note of a phenomenon that had become increasingly apparent in the course of that election year, particularly in the aftermath of the Democrats' Chicago convention. The press is becoming a victim of the increasing political polarization that strains the fabric of our society today. The greater the polarization and the more bitter the antagonisms, the less credit any opponent gives the "neutral" observer and the critical eye—the role the press has long claimed for itself, however well or ill the role has been played. This seems to be true from the demonstrator in the street to the policeman who clashes with him, from third-party candidates to those who hold and exercise the power and responsibility of national government. The more passionate political groups and persuasions, whether they be for civil rights, peace in Vietnam, or law and order, look upon the press with mistrust and hostility. References by Black Power groups to the "white" press, by white radical groups to the "Establishment" press, and on the Right side of the spectrum, to the "liberal" press, tell the story, and reporters covering the activities of such groups find suspicion, contempt, and outright hostility increasingly their lot. The public at large has been infected by the antipress virus:

According to the same *Newsweek* article, hostility toward the press, always a visceral element in radical politics, has become more and more apparent at the political center and among the great masses of essentially nonpolitical Americans. When Agnew called on the "silent majority" to express their feelings to the networks, calls and letters favoring the Vice President's position considerably exceeded those backing the networks, even in the hotbed of eastern liberals, New York City. In much of the rest of the country it was simply no contest. A subsequent attack by the Vice President on the nation's newspapers in general, and on *The New York Times* and the Washington *Post* in particular, was also a winner across the nation, though not so overwhelmingly popular as his blast at television news.

For the purpose of analysis, one can separate attacks on the press into two categories: (1) criticism of the integrity of the press in pursuing its own stated objectives and (2) rejection of the objectives themselves. In the first, reporters do not get the full story, do not understand it, or willfully distort it. In the second, reporters and their organizations are asked to be "the handmaidens of government," are expected to "get on the team," and are requested, especially in the case of television, to delay and even censor news in the interests of "civic responsibility." In a great many cases, however, the categories are not easily separated, and allegations of the first are often motivated by the demands of the ideological interests that want the press to flatter and promote their own special visions and projects. People in general want the press to tell it like they think it should be. And there undoubtedly remains in the public psyche a vestige of the reaction of societies in ancient times toward messengers who brought bad news—the stock in trade of contemporary journalism. It may be that the American people themselves are growing weary of democracy. Such a reaction to turbulent, uncertain times and seemingly insurmountable problems is not without historical precedent. If such is the case, a growing suspicion of and impatience with the institution of the free press would very likely be an early warning symptom.

But another component of the threat, one that greatly nourishes the others, comes from within the institution of the press itself, from its own corruptions and shortcomings: the trends toward monopoly and conglomeration, which decrease both true diversity and the genuine independence of the press; the control of journalists and their work by business and stage managers and the corruption of journalistic values by those of show-biz and the profit margin; the inadequacy of many reporters and editors to handle the increasingly complex and volatile issues of our age; a widespread lack of professional consciousness and professional responsibility in a system that does not give such values its highest reward priorities; the interlocking tyrannies of "hard" (superficial) news and speed (the value of being first even at the expense of accuracy); in general, the failure of much of the press to live up to and keep up with its own responsibilities.

American journalism has grown a good deal in recent years in the ability, intelligence, and education of its practitioners, in its general level of professionalism, and, of course, in technology; and if nonprofessional interests are no less in control of the institution, they at least tend to evidence that control somewhat less blatantly than was once the case. The critical factor, however, is the *relative* competence of the press with respect to the demands made upon it by contemporary society. The truth is that compared with the past, it may make a very good showing, but its performance has fallen seriously behind the requirements and responsibilities of the present day. While many aspects of our society have experienced virtual revolutions, the press has evolved improvements on techniques and practices which were already aging in 1930. It is still woefully behind in dealing with the problems raised by its own changing technology and degree of impact.

■ CHAPTER 1 ■

The New Weaponry

On the third of January, 1961, the United States severed diplomatic relations with Cuba. The final cause of the break, according to the generally well informed *New York Times,* "was a new propaganda offensive from Havana charging that the U.S. was plotting an 'imminent invasion' of Cuba, and a demand that the U.S. cut its Havana embassy to eleven." The *Times* writer continued, "The Castro Government has become increasingly shrill with its anti-American propaganda to busy minds that otherwise would be preoccupied with dissatisfactions at home." Such was the line; its source was the White House and the State Department. Such egregious insult, such patent lying, was more than our national pride and self-respect—already affronted by the course the Cuban Revolution had taken—could be expected to bear. But what was the truth?

The truth was that however unhappy Washington was with the Castro Revolution, the United States was hardly being calumnied. The "new propaganda offensive" was little more than the statement and reiteration of hard fact. The United States *was* mounting an invasion of Cuba, had swelled its Havana embassy with Central Intelligence Agency operatives, and was training and equipping anti-Castro exiles at a secret base in Guatemala. President Dwight D. Eisenhower had bought the plan in 1960 and had already set up the machinery, the key factor of which was the Retalhuleu training base. The story had begun to seep out by November, 1960, that a big base with an airstrip for handling jets was in operation in Guatemala, which had no jets. By the time the lame-duck Republican Administration broke relations with Cuba on January 3, it was clear from the Castro government's "shrill . . . anti-American propaganda" about invasion plans that the Cubans were well aware of at least a good part of what was going on. Definitive proof of that came on April 17, 1961, when the invaders waded ashore and into the open sights of the Cuban Army.

Less than a month after the bloody fiasco at the Bay of Pigs President John F. Kennedy castigated the press in general and *The New York Times* in particular for what he called premature disclosures of security information. The occasion was a White House meeting with the nation's top news executives. Yet at the same meeting Kennedy is also said to have remarked, in an aside to Turner Catledge, then managing editor of the *Times:* "If you had printed more about the operation, you would have saved us from a colossal mistake." Much later, Kennedy told Orvil Dryfoos, then the *Times*'s publisher, "I wish you had run everything on Cuba. . . . I am just sorry you didn't tell it all at the time."

Was the implication of this curious, plaintive turnabout that had the *Times* told all it knew, the operation's security would have been too badly compromised to continue with it, or that the pressure of public opinion at home and the displeasure of allied governments abroad would have forced a cancellation of the project? In an article in the Fall, 1967, issue of the *Columbia University Forum,* "The Press and the Bay of Pigs" (from which the above story is drawn), Victor Bernstein and Jesse Gordon suggest that a cancellation would have been unlikely even if the *Times* had "run everything," and that Kennedy's motivation in his statements to Catledge and Dryfoos was a desire to share a little of the blame for the catastrophe. Bernstein and Gordon may be right; the *Times,* of course, did not find that particular story fit to print. There is, however, one clear implication of Kennedy's hindsight regret: A democratic society is ill and dangerously served when the press is muzzled or chooses to muzzle itself.

Two years later, as the Vietnam problem was beginning to show its remarkable intractability and the public was beginning to grow restive, President Kennedy suggested to the new *Times* publisher, Arthur Ochs Sulzberger, that the *Times*'s Saigon correspondent, David Halberstam, be replaced. Halberstam, soon to share a Pulitzer Prize for his Vietnam reporting, was consistently sending dispatches at great critical and pessimistic variance from the reports the Administration was getting from its own people. The publisher, to his and his paper's credit, rejected the suggestion. But Kennedy, it would seem, had already forgotten the lesson of the Bay of Pigs. If he remembered it when he was finally forced to pull the rug out from under the Ngo Dinh Diem regime, it hasn't been made public. The ambiguous attitude toward the press demonstrated in Kennedy's 1961 colloquy with the news executives perhaps reflected a conflict between Kennedy the intellectual and Kennedy the Chief Executive. But the Chief Executive was dominant, the instinctive reaction when the heat was on; the intellectual was a rueful hindsight in the aftermath of failure. More importantly, his criticism of "premature disclosures" and his effort to remove the nettlesome Halberstam reflected the growing tendency of government in our manipulative age to try to spoon-feed those who put it in office and to turn the press into "the handmaidens of government."

In a representative democracy the people delegate to their elected representatives the power to make and carry out decisions affecting the nation's business but reserve to themselves the right to examine those decisions and review the performance of those elected—not only from election to election but from day to day, from decision to decision, as the provisions for impeachment and congressional review of executive actions both make clear. If, in fact, they could be separated, freedom of the press would have to supersede even freedom of speech in importance to the democratic process, for unless the electorate can be apprised of situations and governmental actions, freedom of speech loses its function in the political process. If the people are not freely and accurately informed, freedom of speech is a small luxury an enlightened dictator might well permit his subjects with little risk to his power. Control over the information the public receives is sufficient to manage what the public thinks, says, and does. And such control is, in any country at any time, the goal of "news management."

Since the beginning of World War II, democratic theory about freedom of the press and actual practice have shown increasingly little resemblance to one another. The instinct of government is not to provide information but to "manage" it, to manipulate the information the public receives in order to elicit a desired response. It would be naïve to think this is not always true of governments and men in power. But the pressures of our security- and managerial-minded age, together with its technological achievements, have transformed what was once a self-protective tendency into a continuing policy with powerful tools available for its implementation.

Discussing the Cuban missile crises of 1962, the then Assistant Secretary of Defense for Public Affairs, Arthur Sylvester, stated that government officials had the right to lie to the public if the nation was in danger of nuclear destruction. Although many might begrudgingly grant Sylvester his point, the record demonstrates that government officials feel they have a right to lie whenever they or their policies can be advanced and/or protected thereby. Sylvester gave his dictum broader, and blunter, application at a later date when he told a group of American reporters in Saigon, "Look, if you think any American official is going to tell the truth, then you're stupid!"* It is a line that merits professional envy and should be carved in large letters alongside "And the truth shall make you free" at the entrance of every school of journalism in the country. During the same highly acrimonious meeting, according to Morely Safer, of CBS, "He went on to the effect that American correspondents had a patriotic duty to disseminate only information that made the United States look good." News (and, obviously, the newsman) is also in the words of Sylvester, "part of the weaponry." But weaponry for use against whom? The fact is that in every major governmental effort in the field of foreign affairs there are two enemies envisioned. One is usually an insurgency, real or imagined; a Communist country; or a combination of the two, real or imagined. The other enemy is the American people themselves

* Morely Safer, "TV Coverage of the War," published in *Dateline,* the publication of the Overseas Press Club, April, 1966.

and the press, whose function it is to inform them. And in the latter battle especially, information is indeed the new weaponry.

The significance of Sylvester's remarks lies not in the uniqueness of the ideas they expressed but, on the contrary, in their representational validity. Sylvester differed from his predecessors, colleagues, and successors not in his approach to the issue but in his expression of it—the fact that he expressed it at all. Ironically, what got Arthur Sylvester in trouble was his candor. He revealed in those comments a basic attitude toward public information (which is to say, toward both the press and the public it informs) which has been a built-in feature of every government agency, from the Central Intelligence Agency to the Federal Communications Commission, of every Administration from Franklin D. Roosevelt to Richard M. Nixon. At its best, the attitude is paternalistic; at its worst, it is contemptuous.

Conflict between the press and the government is, of course, inevitable. The public's right to know, represented by the press, and the government's duty to maintain necessary security are opposing imperatives that provide one of the built-in tensions of any truly democratic system in our complex and difficult world. This tension, this system of opposing responsibilities, when understood and accepted by both government and press and by the society they both serve, is one of the pillars of the democratic process. It is a concrete example of Hegel's conflict of opposite goods. The German philosopher theorized that out of this conflict of opposites, of thesis and antithesis, came a new entity, synthesis. Hegel's synthesis might be described in the present context (though not by Hegel) as the balance between the two opposing forces. A true synthesis in a democratic framework is difficult to conceive, however, even if one accepts the general philosophical precepts of Hegel's dialectical idealism or of the dialectical materialism preached by his apostate student, Karl Marx. But one thing is clear: When government begins to deny the legitimate responsibilities of the press (and has the power to enforce that denial), or when the press begins to distort its own role or to shirk or deny its own duty, then democracy is in serious trouble.

★   ★   ★

During a press conference in Saigon back in the days of Ngo
Dinh Diem, a senior U.S. military officer, asked an embarrassing
question by an American newsman, snapped at the offending
reporter, "Why the hell don't you get on the team!" It was a remark
that betrayed an attitude all too prevalent among military men and
civilian officials: The proper role of the press, particularly in
matters of military and foreign policy, is to act as an arm of
government.

In the book *Mission in Torment* John Mecklin, a journalist by
profession and a former public-affairs officer with the American
embassy in Saigon, tells the story of a World War II press conference in Washington during which President Roosevelt presented a
bothersome reporter with an Iron Cross for his contributions to the
Nazi war effort. Such conflicts were at a minimum in that war,
however, for the simple reason that significant elements of the
democratic system were put in cold storage for the duration. Press
coverage in war theaters was controlled, censorship was imposed,
and the likelihood of stories embarrassing to policy or damaging to
security was tightly limited. Complementing official action, the
press itself more or less voluntarily constricted its own role, and
abetted by the military, which gave them not only uniforms but
officers' ranks and prerogatives to go with them, reporters went to
war more as civilian adjuncts to the Public Information Office than
as representatives of the public's right to know. In the course of half
a century the United States had witnessed a full spectrum: from the
period when the great goblins of American journalism, Messrs.
William Randolph Hearst and Joseph Pulitzer, literally drove a
weak President into an unwanted and unwarranted war, to the
voluntary muzzling of the press in response to the imperatives of
total mobilization.

Restrictions placed on the press during World War II were
probably necessary and were certainly less severe than they might
have been. The old duality was still thawing out, however, when
Senator Joseph McCarthy began to give his name to the decade of
political and intellectual repression which followed the war. It

seems evident now that the timidity of much of the press at that time was due in large part to a hangover from the experience of its wartime relationship with government and men in power. It is equally evident today that although the press in general has largely remembered and reasserted its own imperatives, the memory of that experience still informs the attitudes of many in government and in the military.

After the Japanese surrender in 1945 and an initial period of demobilization the United States entered the period of the Cold War and found itself with a new set of dilemmas. Wartime controls were repealed, and the business of a nominally open democracy resumed, its tools and structures retrieved from wartime storage. The press was free, theoretically, to have at it again; the public, presumably, once again had a right to know. But the postwar period was not a return to prewar America. The nation had, with the rest of the world, been through a profound and affecting experience, one that was to continue through the decade of the fifties. We had become involved, as we still are, with the anomalies of a democracy in a permanent state of semimobilization and nascent warfare. Our system of checks and balances was presided over by an increasingly powerful executive branch, increasingly unbalanced and unchecked, and by powerful, nearly autonomous federal agencies, such as the Department of Defense, the Central Intelligence Agency, the Federal Bureau of Investigation. We were into the age of the "New Caesars,"* an age initiated in the Depression of the thirties, established during the Second World War, and confirmed in the terrible mushrooms that rose over Hiroshima and Nagasaki. Formal declarations of war, an earlier convention that embodied the people's right, through their congressional representatives, to decide questions of war and peace *before* the fact, disappeared in those clouds and in the international situation that followed them. The two most significant accomplishments of modern technology— a destructive power nearly absolute and the speed of delivery and

---

*A phrase suggested by two works of Amaury de Riencourt, *The Coming Caesars* and *The American Empire,* as well as by another phrase increasingly in use by critics (and some friends) of contemporary American foreign policy, "Pax Americana."

communication—had rendered the procedures of representational democracy cumbersome anachronisms. The most critical and far-reaching national decisions were made by one man and his apparatus of *appointed* officials. Security was the order of the day, and secrecy and decisiveness its requirements. The process of representational democracy still functioned, but *after* the fact.

This meant that a President, in most matters of foreign policy requiring either delicacy or force, had to justify his actions to the Congress and to the electorate rather than devise them on the basis of prior consensus. This obvious fact is what made Lyndon Johnson's vaunted concept of consensus politics a total fraud and provided his Administration with a prefabricated credibility gap. On the success (or failure) of such justifications, as Johnson learned, may hang the tenure of the President and the political fortunes of his party. But all too often, as in the case of the Vietnam war, Congress and people have been presented with the purchase of a pig in a poke made in their name, and though they may get rid of the purchasing agent, disposing of the pig is usually a far more difficult matter.

One of the things government has going for it is that the public, conditioned to the new state of things, generally reacts to foreign-policy moves that threaten or include significant American, even military, involvement as being either inevitable or an accomplished fact about the origin of which there is little point in arguing. It is a little bit like selling a product through a mail-order catalog. By the time the buyer has a chance to examine the item, he has either parted with his money or legally obligated himself to do so (often unaware of the nature of the interest and carrying charges). On the other hand, it is difficult to sell a product even through the mails when there are people writing that it is badly made, has a tendency to fall apart after first use, or just doesn't work. A sympathetic, or at least docile, press is of primary importance to the smooth functioning of the new order.

When American forces were reeling backward under the onslaught of the North Korean Army in 1950, few Americans real-

ized just how bad the situation was. Anyone who followed the daily
progress of the "front" on the maps published in most newspapers
knew that it was serious. What they did not know, and were not
told, was that the United States of America, the most powerful
nation in the world, had fielded a military force that was simply
inferior, man for man, to that of its enemy, a military power that
didn't even show on the charts. The problem, to most Americans,
was obviously due to the overwhelming numerical superiority of the
prolific Asians. It was the North Korean "hordes," as later it would
be the Chinese "hordes." It was a view expounded in copious reams
of purple prose written by correspondents near the scene, or near
General Douglas MacArthur's mimeograph machines, and by editorial writers and pundits in the States. And it was a view that
belonged in comic books, not on the pages of American newspapers. In the opinion of one of the war's chief historians, T. R.
Fehrenbach, few conflicts have been so badly reported by modern
journalism:

> Again and again . . . dispatches referred to "wave after
> wave of screaming North Koreans" crashing against American
> lines. Newspaper after newspaper printed the fact that "we are
> still outnumbered at least four to one." Some papers put the
> figure at ten to one. . . . In this, the Army aided and abetted
> them, and did nothing to disillusion them. . . . In actuality,
> the NKPA held a slight superiority in men on 20 July. By 22
> July, U.N. and North Korean forces were on a par, and by the
> end of July United Nations forces actually outnumbered the
> Inmun Gun, an advantage they never again lost. . . . But few
> correspondents saw that officers, giving crucial commands,
> could never be sure if their orders would be obeyed. . . . One
> highly decorated colonel . . . wrote HQ: "I want double the
> TO of officers with each unit—one to lead and the other to
> drive."
>
> Or if they saw, their stories were not printed. A free press is
> equally free to print the truth or ignore it, as it chooses.*

* T. R. Fehrenbach, *This Kind of War* (New York: The Macmillan Company,
1963), pp. 149–151.

But it was not an altogether free press Fehrenbach was criticizing. It had yet to slough off completely its World War II role as nourisher of home-front morale and reassert its independence as provider of facts and representative of the people's right to know. Ernie Pyle was still king-in-image to the working press and their editors: compassionate, fearless, and an utterly dedicated propagandist for the national cause—very much "on the team." And though the first two elements of that image may not always have been emulated by reporters covering the Korean conflict, the third, at least at the beginning, was adhered to rather assiduously.

It took another decade for the thaw to complete itself. The phenomenon of McCarthyism began to expire; the monolithic glacier of the Cold War began to break up, at least to some extent; the authoritarian wartime relationship between the government and the people began to dissolve; dissent and the clash of ideologies became almost respectable again. And new blood, undisciplined by and contemptuous of the subservience of news to policy, emerged from colleges and universities to join the staffs of the nation's newspapers, magazines, and broadcasting news departments.

By the end of the fifties these changes began to uncover an emerging dichotomy that made conflict inevitable: a reinvigorated press on the one hand, increasingly jealous of its prerogatives and reasserting its independence from government and policy, and on the other hand, a governmental establishment still steeped in the essentially totalitarian concepts of wartime, an orientation reenforced by powerful new trends toward a managed democracy on all levels of national life. It is both ironic and illustrative that this conflict surfaced most dramatically during an Administration blessed with greater intellect, a greater sense of history, and a greater appreciation of the countervailing value of a free press to the democratic form of government than any in recent history: that of John F. Kennedy.

If Korea and the Bay of Pigs reflected an older relationship between press and government, Vietnam, almost simultaneously with the Cuban episodes, began to express a new one, a relationship more adversary than cooperative. And on the Vietnam story the old and the new relationships themselves, as they were embodied in the personalities and attitudes of working journalists, collided dramatically. By 1963 the hostility between the government and much of the press over Vietnam coverage was paralleled by another conflict—the bitter clash between the generation of Ernie Pyle, Joseph Alsop, and Maggie Higgins and the generation of David Halberstam, Charles Mohr, and Peter Arnett. The former accused the latter of everything from incompetence to treason; it was essentially an echo of the demand to "get on the team!"

■ CHAPTER 2 ■

Management and Manipulation

There are two interrelated methods by which government seeks to shape and guide the consciousness of its electorate. The first is by control of access to information about its agencies and activities. The second is its positive efforts to disseminate information the content and tone of which it is the author. The first is called security; the second has to be called propaganda. American broadcasting stations cannot, by law, carry radio or television programs produced by the United States Information Agency's broadcast arm, the Voice of America. The reason for this prohibition in legislation establishing U.S.I.A. is clear: The agency was created as an avowed and unabashed official propaganda mechanism of the United States government to combat the powerful and heavily funded propaganda voice of the Soviet bloc; those who sponsored the law understandably rejected the idea that an elected government should use taxpayers' money to propagandize those to whom it is responsible. To apply cosmetics to the face America presents to the rest of the world is one thing: to con the electorate with its own money is quite another.

Unfortunately, this otherwise commendable effort was like patching one hole in a sieve. The amount of taxpayers' money any given Administration spends on efforts to propagandize the electorate is prodigious indeed—estimated at 400 million dollars annually*—and a very interesting congressional investigation might

* The figure is cited for the year 1967 by William Rivers and Wilbur Schramm in *Responsibility in Mass Communication*, rev. ed. (New York: Harper & Row,

12

be held into the question of whether the government spends more money projecting our image abroad or in selling the desired image of itself to the American people. The number alone of people employed by the various major agencies, including the military, in the business of "public information" would astonish many and provide a skeletal index of the magnitude of this effort. "Public information," like "public relations," is simply a bureaucrats' euphemism for propaganda.

Self-serving statements to the public by elected officials concerning their conduct of the public's business have always been a commonplace and expected part of the political scene. They are generally recognized and accepted by the voter with the same combination of indulgence and skepticism with which he greets a salesman's pitch. It is an almost honest form of propaganda, full of lies and half-truths though it may be, related in spirit to the rhetoric of election campaigns; indeed, it is part of the continuous process of campaigning. But this is only the tip of the propaganda iceberg. The greater mass of internally directed propaganda activity ranges across a full spectrum, from writing official handouts to be used in (and sometimes *as*) news stories, through enacting carefully choreographed "inspection" tours for Congressmen, to the planting of wholly false information and the actual fabrication of events to prove a point.

The security system is at the heart of this propaganda effort. When the press is denied access to sources, the only information available to the public is what the government wishes it to know. During the ABM dispute the Pentagon unveiled previously classified information concerning the Russian missile effort to be used as an argument for the Administration's case while keeping the security wraps on other intelligence data that argued to the contrary.

Publishers, 1969), p. 97. The authors describe the significance of that figure by observing that "the executive branch, in fact, spends more on publicity, news, views, publications, and special pleadings than is spent to operate the entirety of the legislative and judicial branches. All together, federal expenditures on telling and showing the taxpayers are more than double the combined costs of news gathering by the two major U.S. wire services, the three major television networks, and the ten largest American newspapers. All this dwarfs the similar efforts of state and municipal governments, but they, too, are convinced of the need for engineering consent."

Chemical and biological warfare (CBW) has long been one of the most sensitive subjects in the classified closet, and until recently military officials declined even to mention the subject. But the sensitivity varied, not according to any national security require- ments, but according to the public-relations situation and the needs of the program for more money or less publicity. During the first part of the 1960's the Army's Chemical Corps conducted a massive promotional campaign to sell CBW to the American people and to the Congress. Officials became closemouthed about CBW as public reaction to news of the program became increasingly negative.* In March, 1968, approximately six thousand sheep in Skull Valley, Utah, suddenly lay down and died. The cause of death proved to be exposure to a nerve gas from the Army's nearby Dugway proving ground, where CBW agents are tested. The Army, however, lied in its teeth, denying what it knew to be perfectly true, that its nerve gas had killed the sheep. It persisted in its denial, curiously, even after it had agreed to indemnify the owners of the animals. Not until May, 1969, was a spokesman for the Chemical Corps forced to admit to a House subcommittee that it had lied all along.

The selective use of classified information also frequently charac- terizes the relationship between government officials and individual reporters and news organizations. Access, partial access, or prior access is often given to reporters and columnists who officials feel can be relied upon to handle sensitive stories in a "responsible" manner. This practice is, in effect, a conditioning mechanism—a carrot-and-stick approach to the press. In short, the "good guys" often get the initial interviews, the leaks, the first information on a major story; and in the news business, being first is almost more important than being right. As a result, there is far more subter- ranean psychological control by government officials over what appears on the pages of American newspapers and on its television screens than most readers and viewers might imagine—and many journalists will admit, even to themselves.

It is in the area of foreign policy in general, and in particular the issue of the Vietnam war, that the situation most clearly reveals

---

* See Seymour M. Hersh, *Chemical and Biological Warfare* (Indianapolis: The Bobbs-Merrill Company, Inc., 1968).

itself. Indeed, Vietnam has become a veritable laboratory for the study of the internally directed propaganda machine, the relationship of government to the press, and the manner in which government attempts, not always unsuccessfully, to use the press as a weapon in its war on the public's awareness.

The Other Enemy

A man from Mars admitted to official inner circles in both Vietnam and Washington could have been excused if he got the impression that the newsmen, as well as the Viet Cong, were the enemy.

—John Mecklin, *Mission in Torment*

On January 2, 1963, there occurred one of the most significant battles of the Vietnam war. Larger battles, many of them, have occurred in that war since, battles fielding far more troops on both sides: Ia Drang, Dak To, Khe Sanh, Hue, even Saigon itself, are place names for battles involving far greater numbers of troops and of far greater military significance in the conventional sense. But the battle of Ap Bac retains its place in the history of that war, if only for having dramatically demonstrated the foolishness of applying conventional measurements to an essentially guerrilla conflict as well as the great dangers in store for those who fall into the trap of believing their own propaganda and of accepting as intelligence the self-advertisement and wishful thinking of those around them.

The battle of Ap Bac has been chronicled before by several writers: Neil Sheehan and David Halberstam, from personal observation on the scene; Bernard Fall, Kuno Knoeble, and Wilfred Burchett, after the fact. As for official descriptions in the aftermath of the battle, that of the National Liberation Front itself was the only one that approached reality. Ordinarily, N.L.F. accounts of events in Vietnam are "pure" propaganda and relate to the facts only when the facts are useful (perhaps a national characteristic, for the South Vietnamese do much the same). Here, however, the simple unadorned truth was all that the most ardent propagandist could ask for.

Ap Bac is a Mekong Delta village about forty miles southwest of

Saigon, in the province of Kien Tuong. The village itself held little
or no strategic value, but two factors combined to give it particular
importance: (1) The insurgents were at this time steadily increasing the areas under their control, inching ever closer to the capital
city, and (2) reports had it that Ap Bac had recently been occupied
by the N.L.F.'s 514th Battalion, an elite unit that had been playing havoc with South Vietnamese forces in the area. It seemed to be
a chance for the South Vietnamese and their American advisers to
pluck a significant psychological, as well as military, plum. As
David Halberstam has described it:

> The mercurial elusiveness of the Viet Cong had become more
> and more exasperating and frustrating to the American advisers.
> Over and over again one heard the same sentence (which was to
> change as the Viet Cong became stronger): *If we could only
> make them stand and fight.* The U.S. military were desperately
> eager for a traditional set-piece battle into which they could
> throw the Government's vastly superior material resources.
> . . . Ap Bac was to be as close to a golden opportunity as
> there ever was in Vietnam; instead, it was a battle which demon-
> strated on a grand and dramatic scale all the tiny failings of
> the system, all the false techniques, evasions and frauds which
> had marked the war in Vietnam.*

What happened was that a secret operation against the 514th
was organized, a "secret" operation that the N.L.F. knew about,
apparently, almost as soon as it was conceived. The attack on Ap
Bac, against a battalion amounting to less than half the strength of
an equivalent South Vietnamese unit, was mounted by a full regiment from the Seventh Vietnamese Division (three battalions),
with a large force of paratroopers held in reserve. In addition, the
attacking force boasted the "vastly superior material resources" the
Americans so wanted to employ: fighter-bombers, helicopters, and
APC 113's (tracked, armored personnel carriers ideally suited for
crossing swamps and inundated rice paddies, which make up so
large a portion of the delta countryside). The outcome, in brief,

* David Halberstram, *The Making of a Quagmire* (New York: Random House,
Inc., 1964), p. 147.

was that the South Vietnamese attack, after hours of air and artillery bombardment, met a well dug-in enemy willing and anxious to fight, superbly disciplined and led. The assault force, on the other hand, had neither motivation, discipline, nor leadership. Its officers either refused to advance after the first repulses or abandoned their commands altogether. Senior officers, out of political considerations, failed to block the escape route of their nearly encircled enemy and out of sheer incompetence and confusion shelled their own men. In the end, an operation mounted for the sole purpose of trapping and destroying a main-force N.L.F. battalion had not only failed, by allowing that battalion to escape, but had suffered 61 dead and 123 wounded while inflicting only 24 dead and 17 wounded on its enemy. All that wonderful hardware did them little good, and much of it was left to rust in the rice paddies surrounding the village.

When South Vietnamese troops entered the village the following day, they found just what their exasperated American advisers knew they would find—nothing. The 514th was not only long gone but had taken with it its wounded, all but three of its dead, and had even collected its empty brass cartridges for refilling and use on another day. The Americans couldn't get their South Vietnamese pupils to load their own dead on helicopters.

What followed was a series of the Alice-in-Wonderland performances that so stud the history of the Vietnam war. As if to punctuate the debacle, a South Vietnamese officer ordered the village shelled and succeeded in killing five and wounding fourteen of his own men, very nearly bagging the senior American military adviser and a pair of American reporters in the process. Two other newsmen, Halberstam and Peter Arnett, of the Associated Press, who had been circling the village in a helicopter, returned shortly after this incident to the operation's command post, where they found General Paul Harkins, commander of American forces in Vietnam, about to return to Saigon.

> We asked him what was happening. "We've got them in a trap," he said, "and we're going to spring it in half an hour." We looked at him, completely bewildered. The enemy was

long gone, the Government troops were so completely dis-
organized that they would not even carry out their own dead,
a province chief was shelling his own men—and a trap was
about to be sprung? As on many other occasions in Vietnam,
we never knew whether Harkins believed what he was saying,
or whether he felt it should be said.*

Later, General Harkins and his boss, Admiral Harry Felt, both
described the battle as "a Vietnamese victory, not a defeat, as the
papers say." That it was a Vietnamese victory could hardly be
contested, as Vietnamese played on both sides. Felt punctuated his
own performance by snapping at Neil Sheehan. Sheehan, who was
then covering Vietnam for United Press International, had been on
the scene and was one of those who narrowly missed death when
the village had been shelled. He had, of course, filed what he had
seen and what the American advisers had told him, and the result
had been shock and dismay in Washington, where the line was that
things were going very well in Vietnam. In one of the more
memorable recent examples of "doublespeak" the Admiral told the
reporter: "You ought to talk to some of the people who've got the
facts."

There were others who should have talked to people who had the
facts. They were the members of the 514th N.L.F. Battalion, who
clearly were unaware of the defeat they had suffered. So unaware
were they that a week later they returned to Ap Bac, flew N.L.F.
flags from the rooftops, and sent a letter to General Huynh Van
Cao, the South Vietnamese commander of the region, daring him
to come back and try his luck again. Cao refused. He entered the
village only after a month, with a force of five thousand men, and
again found nothing.

If the battle of Ap Bac was significant for revealing the military,
political, and psychological weaknesses of the South Vietnamese
government and the American policy toward them, the flap that
ensued from reporters' accounts of the action was significant in
exposing the pattern and sources of conflict between the press and
officialdom both in Saigon and Washington—a conflict that was to

* *Ibid.,* p. 155.

grow with the magnification of the war and the deterioration of the South Vietnamese political scene.

The *major* source of this conflict was, and is, a will to deception, both consciously and unconsciously expressed, on the part of officials. Mecklin described the attitude of American officials in Saigon as follows:

> For some officials of the U.S. Mission, misleading a newsman was almost instinctive, if only as a way to get rid of him. . . . They seemed to regard a journalist as a natural adversary who was deliberately trying to sabotage the national interest, or as a child who would not understand and should not be asking about grown-up affairs in any case.

He added the following qualification: "To the best of my knowledge, no responsible U.S. official in Saigon ever told a newsman a really big falsehood, instead there were endless little ones. They were morally marginal and thus difficult to dispute." There are any number of reporters who have covered Vietnam who would take serious issue with the first part of that qualification, but in the main the small lie, the marginal prevarication, and the misleading statement have been the dominant tactics used by officials in the Information War. But lies, large *or* small, to reporters represent only a part of the problem, and perhaps not the largest part. A more significant part of the problem, of which much of the conflict with the press is only a visible symptom, is the tendency of the great political-military bureaucracy involved in Vietnam to deceive itself. Like the lies of officials and functionaries to the press, this process of misinformation is a concatenation of small deceits by individuals and individual agencies and departments which gathers both magnitude and momentum as it rises from the military commander and civilian representative in the field to the polished desks of the State Department and the Pentagon. This dangerous tendency within the bureaucracy itself had been laid bare at the Bay of Pigs. But that debacle was only a dress rehearsal for what was to come in Vietnam, where in 1963 an additional factor intensified the disease. Mecklin wrote of that period:

We were stuck hopelessly with what amounted to an all-or-nothing policy, which might not work. Yet it *had* to work, like a Catholic marriage or a parachute. The state of mind in both Washington and Saigon tended to close out reason. The policy of support for Diem became an article of faith, and dissent became reprehensible.

In its dealings with newsmen, the U.S. Mission thus was often wrong about the facts, in a situation of utmost importance to the U.S. national interest, in support of a controversial policy that was costing the lives of American servicemen.

Mecklin was writing essentially about the policy of support for the Diem regime. But his capsule analysis applies to our overall involvement in Vietnam with more clarity and precision than any single paragraph on the subject I have ever seen.

It is one of the truisms of our times, detailed several years ago by C. Northcote Parkinson, that bureaucracies develop egos and a will to live of their own, independent of, and at times even contrary to, the ends they originally were created to serve. In composite bureaucracies, whether they be city governments or the massive White House–State Department–Pentagon complex that operates America's foreign policies, the same holds true for the individual parts. As a result, we not only find the various agencies of a single bureaucracy working at cross purposes to one another and athwart the purposes of the institution as a whole, but we also find each step on the hierarchical ladder trying to "sell" itself and its accomplishments to those above it, very much as the bureaucracy itself, be it a city, state, or federal government, tries to sell the electorate. The unadorned, factual report, even within a single establishment, is a very rare phenomenon.

This corruption of the reporting function of bureaucratic units is disastrous to the gathering of intelligence on which policy decisions are made and, not unnaturally, frequently leads to disastrous policies. In addition, a policy, once adopted at the top, tends to elicit reports from subordinate persons and agencies which prove the correctness of the policy and, coincidentally, the wisdom of its architects. The subordinate usually confines his efforts to selling his and his agency's accomplishments within the framework of the policy handed down to him. His function is to make the policy work, period, and his reports to his superiors tend, at the very least, to emphasize those facts and figures which would seem to prove he is doing this successfully and to underplay or ignore those that might call into question the intelligence of the policy itself.

Thus, as the new catchphrase for U.S. Vietnam policy under Richard Nixon became "Vietnamization of the war," there predictably followed a veritable flood of official reports demonstrating rapid progress in the morale and combat efficiency of South Vietnamese fighting units. And again, newsmen who devoted time to covering the phenomenon found their files at dismaying odds with the picture drawn by official reports. The latter, according to *The New York Times*'s Tom Buckley, originated with U.S. advisers in the field. Buckley wrote that for these officers, many of them careerists,

> there is little chance to make a glowing record as an adviser. Most try to make the best of a bad deal, avoiding friction with their Vietnamese counterparts. . . . Meanwhile, they tell headquarters what they think it wants to hear—which at the moment is that the Vietnamese armed forces are rapidly improving. A senior officer admitted to me that this was often the case. "There's a natural feeling among advisers that they're being rated on performance of their units [South Vietnamese units they advise]," he said.*

"Vietnamization" may be a new policy, but "telling headquarters what it wants to hear" is one of the verities that provide continuity in the development of American policy in Vietnam. In an account published following a trip to Vietnam in 1967, William J. Lederer provided another insight into the process and how it works on an individual level. Lederer had run across widespread corruption and theft in the handling of U.S. funds and supplies by Vietnamese Army officers in I Corps. He brought up the situation with an unnamed colonel, who was the senior American adviser to the I Corps headquarters in Danang. He met first with angry

* Tom Buckley, *The New York Times Magazine,* October 12, 1969.

denials, then with a pathetic plea from the officer ("Let's be civilized. Don't put the finger on me."), and finally, an explanation from one of the colonel's aides:

> "What in the hell did you do to the colonel yesterday? I was with him at the club last night. He bent on a beauty. He said you have put him in a double bind. If he tries to persuade General Lam and his staff to be more honest, then General Lam will write to General Westmoreland, and the colonel will get kicked out of his job. And if you write newspaper articles about what's happening here, it might start an investigation. The colonel said that everyone is doing as good a job as is possible under the circumstances. . . . Right now he's up for general. . . . The surest way for him not to get promoted is by trying to reform the Vietnamese corruption. That would kill the colonel's career."*

To make matters worse, there seems to be a perverse dynamic involved which hardens and locks-in policies in direct proportion to their inadequacies and the challenges they receive from outside critics.

American policy in Vietnam, until the fall of Diem in late 1963, was dubbed by one reporter, "Sink or swim with Ngo Dinh Diem." Only variations on the personality (and, if you like, the rhyme) separate the policies of then and now. I was afforded an eye-opening insight into the Byzantine workings of the process shortly after the beginning of my first stay in Vietnam, in the spring of 1966. The Buddhist crisis of that year had just begun to develop into a serious political problem. General Nguyen Chanh Thi, the flamboyant, highly popular, and even more highly independent commander of I Corps, the northernmost of Vietnam's four tactical zones, had just been sacked by his former protégé, Nguyen Cao Ky, and the more militant Buddhists under the enigmatic Thich Tri Quang had decided to make this act the focus of a number of grievances against and demands on the military junta Ky headed. The development contained elements disturbing in the extreme to Vietnamese and American officials alike: It was a disruptive move-

* Quoted by William J. Lederer, *Our Own Worst Enemy* (New York: W. W. Norton & Company, Inc., 1968), p. 216.

ment that threatened to impair national unity, such as it was, and the war effort; it threatened to topple the Ky regime, behind which once again the United States had thrown all its support; it seemed evident that some Vietcong infiltration and influence was involved. But most important, it threatened to mobilize and fan the flames of pacifism in South Vietnam—a desire for peace at almost any price, which in this reporter's opinion was and is the single political sentiment that a vast majority of the Vietnamese people could agree on.

Washington clearly was presented with a difficult problem. An essentially non-Communist movement, the same one that had been the motive force in pulling down the Diem regime, was now demanding the removal of Ky and the junta, the holding of free elections, and at first inferentially but more and more explicitly, an end to the war and to American presence in Vietnam. If the United States felt it had any choice to make at all, that choice had to rest on the answer to two questions: Was the Buddhist movement, in fact, an N.L.F. Trojan horse? And how much support did it have among the people—how successfully had it created, intensified, or mobilized disaffection with the current regime? The answer to the latter question from American officials in Saigon, with all their money on Ky, was defensive of the incumbent regime. The answer to the first question was that the Buddhists' demands would lead to negotiations with the N.L.F., and Washington at that time was not interested in negotiations in any form.

What was the political clout of the militants? During this period I met a young employee of the U.S. Agency for International Development (USAID) in Saigon, whose duties included preparation of the "Presidential telegram," a weekly report to the White House, outlining the political and economic situation across the country and the progress, or lack of it, of USAID activities. This young man's job was to collect and collate reports arriving in Saigon from the agency's representatives in the provinces and to compose from them the first draft of the report. It should be noted that he did not work alone on this but was one of several employees and officials with the same collective function. At one point during the earlier stages of the crisis, reports from the provinces were singularly disheartening, especially from the northern provinces and from the urban areas. The information from the sweltering countryside was collected and processed on the ground floor of the air-conditioned office building on Le Van Duyet Street, in Saigon, and a draft of the report was composed and sent upstairs for the signature or the corrections of the USAID director. It came back with a note to the effect that it was far too pessimistic to send to the President and had to be redone. Like a yo-yo, the report vertically traversed the building several times before the director was sufficiently satisfied to send it out over his signature. Needless to say, the report received in Washington that day bore little, if any, relationship to the message the people in the field were trying to get through.

Precisely what effect such "optimized" reports had in Washington is impossible to assess. But it is evident that they tended to downgrade the political support the movement had and, consequently, its political importance. This is just what U.S. officials were trying to fob off on reporters, but without much success. In any event, Washington decided to back Ky and the complete suppression of the militant Buddhists all the way. And suppressed they were, broken, scattered, imprisoned; any threat they posed to the junta and American policy was effectively ended. But not all Americans in Saigon at the time were completely elated with the result. One high-ranking U.S. official, by no means friendly to Tri Quang and his followers, worried aloud one day about the long-range implications of Ky's success. The Buddhists, he observed, constituted the only genuine mass political movement, in the modern sense of the word, that could possibly compete with the N.L.F. on the political level. Their destruction, as a movement, might well leave a vacuum that could only be filled by the military in a state of war.

Though never openly expressed by officials in Washington or Saigon, this fear began to look like prophecy as 1968 expired and 1969 progressed. President Nguyen Van Thieu, whose election in 1967 meant little more than the "legitimization" of military control of the government in force since the overthrow of Diem, urged the formation of a "loyal opposition" out of one corner of his mouth while out of the other he ordered the imprisonment of effective oppositionists, such as the runner-up in the presidential elections, Truong Dinh Dzu. The various opposition groups that do exist find their efforts to organize an opposition coalition frustrated both by their own mistrust of one another and by intimidation from the government. Speaking to a reporter in October, 1969, the leader of one such group expressed the general belief that Thieu would never allow an effective opposition to form. "If you want to learn about the status of the non-Communist opposition, go to Con Son," he told a visitor recently, referring to a prison island off the coast. "That's where you'll find the largest gathering." The politician, a leader of the Hoa Hao sect, also explained that what room for maneuver oppositionists possessed in Saigon was due largely to the presence of large numbers of newsmen in the capital and was not reflected in the provinces, where "the province chiefs take it upon themselves to police our people very closely."*

In mid-November, 1969, the Thieu Government released the text of a "captured Communist document" that called for the overthrow of the Government via a political offensive utilizing tactics currently in use by the non-Communist opposition leaders. The implication was clear to the Vietnamese politicos. Whether the document was real or a Government fabrication, they felt it was being used in yet another effort to further intimidate opposition efforts, and quite possibly to prepare the ground for some additions to the population of Con Son.

The American position, publicly, and at least until Nixon took over the reins, was to encourage the Thieu Government to "broaden the base" of its support. In the words of W. Averell Harriman, "We've been urging Thieu to broaden the base, and he did to some extent when he brought in Tran Van Huong last year as Premier, and then others, but he didn't really bring together a coalition of all the anti-Vietcong forces."† Unfortunately, even the small blessing the popular and respected Huong represented was short-lived. He was subsequently fired and replaced with a general, Tran Thien Khiem, a military crony of the President. Three years after the Constituent Assembly elections of 1966, South Vietnam remains without the basic ingredient of political democracy: effective oppo-

---

* Quoted by Terence Smith, *The New York Times,* October 25, 1969.

† W. Averell Harriman, quoted in *The New York Times Magazine,* August 24, 1969.

sition parties. Thieu has thus far ruled out the necessary basis for
success in Paris by refusing to consider any direct Communist participation in the political affairs of South Vietnam and by explicitly
rejecting the idea of a pre-election coalition arrangement. The idea
of a "third force," a new government that would be more flexible
toward the N.L.F., was thought by some to be seriously compromised when Hanoi and the N.L.F. began to urge the idea. But
that was naïve; the "third force" was buried in the rubble of the
Buddhist uprising of 1966. If Truong Dinh Dzu were elected to-
morrow, he would be forced to follow Thieu's path or be over-
thrown in a week. If such a reminder of South Vietnam's sorry
political state were needed, it was provided by Vice President Ky
when he warned, on September 13, 1969, that any attempt to
form a coalition with the N.L.F. would be answered by a military
coup "inside ten days."

As the history of Latin America should suffice to teach us, no
nation can seriously (or for long) call itself a democracy if elected
civilian political organizations cannot control the nation's military.
And no political organization can do so unless it possesses a truly
strong mass base and mass organization. There is no such political
organization today in South Vietnam, and all hopes of developing
one have been systematically crushed by the South Vietnamese military with the connivance, or at least the genial sufferance, of the
Americans. That is what has become of our vaunted pledge to
permit the Vietnamese people to choose their own form of government and to protect their ability to do so. That is also why President Nixon, perhaps, finds his only alternatives to be prolongation
of the war at a diminished rate of American participation, or capitulation. The *political* answer to the National Liberation Front has
been strangled.

The United States may well find, therefore, as it continues to
grapple with the problems of negotiations in Paris to end the war
and to move the conflict from the military to the political arena,
that it sowed the wind in 1966 and is about to reap the biblical
harvest: "For they have sown the wind, and they shall reap the
whirlwind: it hath no stalk: the bud shall yield no meal: if so be it
yield, the strangers shall swallow it up [Hosea 8:7]."

■ CHAPTER 3 ■

Déjà Vu

*But the point made early in the . . . crisis by some Americans
. . . was that the United States tended prematurely to put all its
eggs in one basket.*

*But soon these briefings developed into occasionally bitter and
always frustrating contests between the newsmen who wanted to
know what was really happening and the spokesmen who were not
authorized to divulge this to them. . . . [The briefings] were an
important part of the whole picture of misleading newsmen and,
through them, public opinion about what the United States was
doing or planning to do.*

*It was seemingly another case of the President's being fed
exaggerated and inaccurate information which he accepted in good
faith.*

These passages describe the critical aspects of the Vietnam story
and the dilemma facing the newsmen who cover it as aptly and succinctly as any previously quoted. But they weren't written with
Vietnam in mind at all. They are taken from Tad Szulc's excellent
book, *Dominican Diary,* a blow-by-blow account of the massive
American intervention of 1965—a year and six months after the
overthrow of that other overloaded basket, Ngo Dinh Diem, and
almost simultaneous with the beginning of the massive introduction
of American ground forces which that policy had led to.

Although in many fundamental respects the Dominican and

27

Vietnamese situations were vastly different, the workings of American policy formation, intelligence analysis, and information practices in the two situations are astonishing in the number and precision of their correspondencies. And although Vietnam remains the laboratory offering the greatest scope and detail for examining Washington's handling of public information and its treatment of the press, the events in Santo Domingo from April through August of 1965 are of the greatest importance in demonstrating that the malaise of Vietnam is much more than an isolated situation developing out of a unique set of circumstances.

In December, 1962, a year and a half after the assassination of the dictator Rafael Trujillo, the Dominican people enjoyed their first democratic government in thirty-eight years under the leadership of the newly elected President, Dr. Juan Bosch. But the new democracy was also a very short-lived one. Nine months after it took over, the Bosch government was felled by a military coup composed of officers who were holdovers from the Trujillo regime and who were highly unsatisfied with their diminished roles and the diminishment of the considerable perquisites and emoluments they enjoyed under the dictatorship. For nineteen months after the September, 1963, coup the Dominicans were ruled by a government headed by a civilian, Donald Reid Cabral, but backed and dictated to by a military junta—in any event, a government that was in no sense democratic. Then, on April 24, 1965, another military coup was attempted, this one led by younger officers and with the purpose of returning power to the exiled Bosch and democracy to the Dominican people.

The "coup" quickly became civil war, at least in the capital city of Santo Domingo; and just as quickly, the United States decided it had to act to prevent "another Cuba" from emerging in the Caribbean. The wider background for such a reaction was the institutionalized fear of "Left" movements and parties, particularly in Latin America, even though Right and Left are measured there from a center close to fascism. But a more immediate cause was the exaggerated and inaccurate and often deliberately inflammatory reports sent to Washington by its ambassador in Santo Domingo, W. Tapley Bennett, Jr., a man so out of touch with events in the country that on April 24 he was visiting his mother in Georgia.

On returning to Santo Domingo, Bennett sized up the situation as a Communist-, or at least an "extremist-," led rebellion, and recommended U.S. intervention on the side of the forces led by Brigadier General Elias Wessín y Wessín, the leading figure of the old junta, to prevent a rebel victory as well as for the purpose of evacuating Americans from the country. On Tuesday, April 27, three days after fighting had begun in Santo Domingo's streets, the pro-Bosch forces suffered a heavy blow. The Navy, which they had counted on their side, went over to Wessín, and a regiment from San Cristóbal in the interior, which had been biding its time awaiting the outcome, decided to do the same. Seemingly defeated, the rebels asked Ambassador Bennett to mediate between them and General Wessín's forces for an end to the conflict. According to the man who subsequently emerged as leader of the rebel forces, Lt. Colonel Francisco Caamaño Deño, the U.S. ambassador demanded their surrender. Bennett denies this, but his already all-too-amply expressed attitude toward the rebels lends credence to Colonel Caamaño's version.

U.S. newspapers the following day carried news of the rebel collapse, and officials in Washington, while still maintaining as best they could the fiction of U.S. "neutrality" in the situation, were expressing relief. The relief, however, was premature. What had not been reported to Washington was Caamaño's parting remarks to the American ambassador that the rebels would go on fighting anyhow. And fight they did. By Wednesday evening Bennett was cabling Washington that the situation was deteriorating rapidly and that American lives were in danger. He urged the landing of Marines to evacuate U.S. citizens. On Thursday morning the Marines landed, and thus began the armed intervention of the United States in the Dominican Republic, an intervention that soon was to involve 22,000 American troops ashore and another 1,100 or more in air and sea support of them. Junta forces had been on the verge of collapse, but they were saved, and the civil war prolonged by four months, by the timely intervention of the U.S. Marines and elements of the 82nd Airborne Division on their behalf.

At 8 P.M., Wednesday, April 28—one hour after the Marines, in ships lying offshore, had been given the order to land—Ambassador Bennett again cabled Washington. Junta forces, he said, were breaking down and were

> incapable of resistance. . . . I recommend that serious thought be given to armed intervention to restore order beyond a mere protection of lives. If the present loyalist [*sic*] efforts fail, the power will go to groups whose aims are identical with those of the Communist Party. We might have to intervene to prevent another Cuba.

Interspersed with such recommendations, and backing them up, was a stream of exaggerated and unfounded reports and rumors about the rebel leadership and rebel atrocities which continued to pour fuel on the fires of panic already burning in the White House. It was a stream that intensified with the remarkable rebel comeback. That event not only spurred a quickening of the flow but was itself used as evidence that Communists and pro-Castro elements were now in command, the thesis being that only they had the discipline and organizational skills to pull it off. (The same kind of poisoned reasoning was to be heard again, almost a year to the day later, when Buddhists took to the streets—and took over a couple of cities—in South Vietnam.) The two most famous of these stories were the horrifying tale of the execution of a junta colonel whose head was removed and carried around town on a pike (the colonel was later found with minor wounds in a hospital) and the lugubrious story, related time and time again by President Johnson, of Tapley Bennett and his secretary cowering under their desks while machine-gun fire raked the American Embassy (an event that never occurred). And most of the press, at this point, was not yet disabused. As Szulc tells it:

> Having no reason at this point to disbelieve the embassy's information, we took copious notes. And again we filed most of this information to our newspapers just as the Ambassador had filed it to the State Department. . . . This whole episode, then, added up to the lesson that one never seems to learn well enough in journalism: do not ever trust anybody's word, no matter how high his position and how good his credentials.

Troops of the 82nd Airborne Division intervened directly and critically on the side of the junta forces immediately after landing. The junta forces, in a rapidly deteriorating condition, were largely confined to the San Isidro Air Base, across the Ozama River from the city, which by now was held almost entirely by the rebels, whose strength continued to grow. Whereas the mission of the Marines was to secure an "international safety zone" surrounding and protecting foreign embassies and ostensibly for the purpose of evacuating foreigners, the mission of the paratroopers was to secure the Duarte Bridge across a river outside the zone, thereby blocking any rebel move on the junta's forces at San Isidro. American officials, both in Washington and in Santo Domingo, were still insisting that the United States was neutral. Three days later, the paratroopers moved out from their newly acquired positions on the city side of the bridge to open a "security corridor" that linked the Marines in the safety zone with the army command at San Isidro. In military parlance such a corridor is called a line of communication. In military reality *this* line of communication conveniently and effectively cut the rebel territory in half and surrounded its main stronghold, in the city's business district, with American forces. The United States was still neutral.

General Wessín's forces had earlier become the Benoit junta's forces in a rather obvious juggling act that pushed the unpopular General, at least publicly, into the background and brought up Colonel Pedro Bartolomé Benoit as leader of the San Isidro junta. The affair was stage-managed, as later the creation of the Imbert group would be, by the American embassy in order that its protégés might present a more palatable front. The United States was still not interfering in the internal affairs of the Dominican Republic.

Later, during a painfully achieved and tenuously maintained cease-fire, U.S. forces occupied a peace-keeping position—standing between the two antagonists. The junta, however, now led by yet another creation of the U.S. embassy, Brigadier General Antonio Imbert Barreras, was preparing to attack the rebel forces in the northern part of the city. To do this, Imbert's troops had to cross U.S. lines. This they did with no trouble, passing through U.S.–manned checkpoints as American television cameras filmed their progress. Rebel forces in the northern sector hadn't a chance: Largely poorly or untrained irregulars, they were cut off from their center of strength downtown by the paratroopers' security corridor and, of course, from any chance of resupply and reenforcement— even from adequate communication with their command—for while junta forces could cross American lines, rebel forces could not. The result was general slaughter, not only of rebel forces in the area but of inhabitants as a whole. In several instances reporters covering the battle found American officers and radio teams accompanying the junta troops; at one point they observed U.S. troops delivering rations to the attackers. But the United States was still neutral, was "not cooperating" with General Imbert's forces. Lieutenant General Bruce Palmer, commander of U.S. military forces in Santo Domingo, explained the regular crossing of U.S. lines by junta troops as "isolated incidents" and "accidents" and contended that U.S. officers had firm orders against assisting either side. In Washington the same story was told. If what Palmer said was true, then the American troops in Santo Domingo must have been the most undisciplined force the United States had fielded since the War of 1812.

In fact, American forces were behaving like a policeman who had stopped a fight, handcuffed *one* of the fighters, and then stood back while his unconstrained opponent beat hell out of him. It would have been, it seems, a sufficiently flagrant outrage *without* the spectacle of the policeman wiping the assailant's brow and fetching him a beer when he got thirsty.

While all this was going on, Washington seemed to be coming around to a less paranoid view of the rebel movement and had begun to work out with Juan Bosch, in Puerto Rico, a possible third alternative: a provisional government headed by a wealthy Dominican landowner named Silvestre Antonio Guzman, who had served as Minister of Agriculture under Bosch. The plan was acceptable to Colonel Caamaño and his rebels, but not to General Imbert, a U.S. puppet who, as one reporter remarked, had begun to pull his own strings. McGeorge Bundy, then Special Assistant to the President for National Security Affairs, was sent to negotiate the settlement. With him, more or less, came Thomas C. Mann, Under Secretary of

State for Economic Affairs, to report back on the Dominican situation. Mann, who both by reputation and record seemed to have a special affinity for military dictatorships (it was he who urged the newly inaugurated Johnson to repeal a Kennedy policy and recognize the junta that overthrew Bosch in 1963), opposed the idea and flew back to Washington ten days in advance of Bundy to torpedo it. Even as Bundy's negotiations were approaching success, he received instructions from Washington that pulled the rug out from under the whole plan. Delivering the *coup de grâce* was a story printed in the Washington *Daily News* alleging that the Dominican Republic's Agricultural Bank, of which Guzman had been a director, had been involved in irregularities to the tune of 75 million dollars. The story, which the paper published without attribution, was supplied by a registered agent of the Reid Cabral government. Worse, it was wholly false. Worse than that, the American embassy and USAID in Santo Domingo, as well as the State Department in Washington, had at the time all the information that proved it false. But the story, so conveniently planted and published, did its work. The Guzman solution was dead, and the killing in Santo Domingo went on.

Through this whole shabby affair, from April 24 onward, the American people had been given a snow job by their government; just as, at times, that government had been snowed by its own officials and factotums in the field. There is an unfortunate tendency in describing such governmental actions to use such euphemisms as "misleading," "misinformation," "credibility gap." For reporters, that tendency is probably due to a fairly deep and traditional sense of respect, a desire to understate—just to be safe—and a desire to tell a particular story without unnecessary impairment of one's ability to cover the next one. However that may be, there is ample evidence in the record of the Dominican intervention that, from Tapley Bennett and General Palmer in the field, through the departments of State and Defense, to the President himself, deliberate and quite calculated lies were told the American public. And there were no "security" issues involved in this instance, no "enemy" to mislead (whatever the rhetoric out of Washington, the rebels knew all too painfully what the United States was doing in Santo Domingo). The target of these lies was public opinion, American and international. Szulc describes it aptly, if rather charitably:

> There was very little resemblance between the realities of Santo Domingo and the picture that the Administration, or some members of it, were painting in Washington for the benefit of public opinion. . . . There was no real unified policy in Washington: each official told what he personally believed and what best seemed to serve the interests of the faction within the Government he represented.

In fact, the only insight into the realities of Santo Domingo the American people received were provided them by reporters on the scene, such as Szulc and his *Times* colleagues; Bernard Collier, of the New York *Herald Tribune;* Dick Valeriani and the late Ted Yates, of NBC; and a handful of others. Perhaps even more important, they provided the only contact with reality that many Administration officials had during the crisis, charitably assuming any of them availed themselves of the service.

Tad Szulc's account provides one small irony too good to pass by. On the morning of Monday, May 10, the 82nd Airborne paraded behind a brass band down the security corridor to the U.S. Embassy. Szulc reported that many people found the performance in poor taste. "Rather bitterly, a Dominican who had long lived in the United States asked, 'Are they playing "Marching Through Georgia" or "We Shall Overcome"?' " What neither the reporter nor the embittered Dominican knew was that the man leading the parade, the 82nd's commanding officer, was none other than the senior American adviser at the glorious battle of Ap Bac, Major General Robert York.

■ CHAPTER 4 ■

The Snow Machine

There is an emotional phenomenon in the attitude of officials toward members of the press wherein the publishing and broadcasting of observed defects in policies is held responsible for the failure of those policies. The underlying assumption is that policy, like a hothouse plant, needs only to be left alone in a properly controlled atmosphere, and it will bear fruit. A pointed example of this emotional phenomenon occurred shortly after the Constituent Assembly elections in South Vietnam, in September of 1966. In a dispatch to *The New York Times* Charles Mohr described the elections as the first fair and honest ones the Vietnamese people had ever had. I had covered that election, and my own view was that they were the most cynically set up and manipulated elections I had ever witnessed. Mohr is a first-rate reporter, one for whom I have a great deal of personal and professional respect, and I was rather astounded to read his article. I thought it a piece of positive thinking, at the very best. Frederick E. Nolting, Jr., former U.S. ambassador to (Diem's) South Vietnam, felt differently, however. In a letter to a subsequent edition of the *Times* Nolting castigated Mohr for implying that *Diem's* elections were not fair and honest —and then went on to charge the *Times* and its Saigon correspondents with the collective responsibility for the overthrow of the Diem regime and the death of Diem and his brother Nhu, the subsequent dispatch of more than 300,000 (by then) American troops to Vietnam, and the casualties (then 100 or more a week) that followed!

As with the duplicity in Santo Domingo, this defensive mechanism operated with the military and civilian planners in Saigon and with the President and his aides and advisers in Washington. And like all defensive mechanisms, it operated at the highest speed and intensity when the facts were most grim. To say, in 1963–1964, for instance, that the South Vietnamese government was losing the war to the Viet Cong was to court an enormous store of wrath, not only from government officials but also from Stateside journalists who were intellectually and emotionally committed to the government's view and its policies.

Thus a number of columnists and reporters in this country—chief among them figures such as Joseph Alsop, Henry Taylor, and Maggie Higgins—bitterly attacked the Saigon press corps (especially its American members) for calumnying Diem and undermining the allied war effort. They were charged with being "soft on Communism" and, in the words of Maggie Higgins, with wanting the Viet Cong to win just to prove they (the reporters) were right. Big guns from all sides were turned on the handful of correspondents working Saigon, from Sylvester at Defense to Nolting in Saigon, from fellow columnists to the editors and publishers of major publications. *Time* magazine scandalized the journalistic profession by printing a scathing repudiation of the work of a press corps that pointedly included two of its own correspondents, Charles Mohr and Mert Perry. Both Mohr and Perry resigned over the article, though *Time* made an effort to placate Mohr, and both later returned to Saigon for other publications—Perry for *Newsweek* and Mohr for *The New York Times*. Few would now care to dispute that the young "pessimists" of the Saigon press corps at that time were proven right by subsequent events. It was precisely the imminence of South Vietnamese collapse, which these reporters were trying to point out, which led to the bombing of North Vietnam, the introduction of more than half a million U.S. troops, and an American casualty figure, both dead and wounded, higher than that of the Korean War.

Though the personalities may have changed since that time, the attitudes of officials toward the press are among the few constants in the ever-changing Vietnamese scene. It is an old courtroom technique to discredit the testimony of a witness by attacking his character. In Vietnam, in order to discredit reporters' copy, a mass character-assassination campaign is conducted, repeated whenever it is deemed necessary, in which the standard picture looks something like this: American reporters in Saigon are young, immature, inexperienced, and irresponsible. They are infatuated with their own importance and with the importance of their personal opinions. They are lazy, cowardly, and clannish. They seldom, if ever, get out of Saigon, and they spend their time in hotel bars lapping up gin-and-tonics and interviewing each other. Their criticism is carping, their judgment uninformed and unsound, their attitudes a product of fashionable cynicism and unconcerned ignorance. They are supercilious, arrogant, rude, and thoughtless. They don't bathe often enough, and they are generally biased against the forces of good. And last, but far from least, they are responsible for all the confusion in the American public about the war and about American policy in Vietnam. They misrepresent, either from incompetence, ill-will, or both, the real situation. They focus on negative trivia at the expense of "the big picture." The credibility gap is all their fault. They are two-bit, half-baked Cassandras who are, on the whole, doing a disservice of almost treasonable proportions to the great American public. In short, they are not "on the team."

The team. What the team concept means is that any American in any proximity to any American operation is honor bound to be a member of the American team, whether as player or water boy. It is a concept that officialdom, both military and civilian (but especially military), tends to take for granted. On the other hand, it is a concept hotly rejected by some reporters (regrettably by far too few) who see their function in a different light. Complicating this dispute in places like Vietnam is the rather provincial tendency of some Americans to consider everyone identifiably non-Oriental as responsible to the same ethic. The conflict is often bitter and sometimes even dangerous, but it is not without its lighter moments.

In the spring of 1966, during the Buddhist demonstrations and riots in Saigon, U.S. military policemen were given orders to clear team members off the streets. To the M.P.'s this simply meant any Americans they ran across. One evening two M.P.'s ran into a

gaggle of reporters and cameramen who were waiting at a major
intersection for the next clash between demonstrators and police.
When told they had to get out of the area because all Americans
were ordered off the streets, some British newsmen replied that they
were not Americans, did not come under the authority of U.S.
military police, and were not going to go. The Americans in the
group immediately followed suit (one of them denying his heritage
in a deep southern drawl), committing an act that would probably
strike Arthur Sylvester as comparable to Peter's denial of Christ.
The puzzled M.P.'s decided to solve the problem by checking
identification cards, but they again met with unanimous refusal.
Being non-Americans all, the reporters were not required to show
U.S. military police anything. One of the principal spokesmen for
the press group was Peter Arnett, of the Associated Press. Arnett,
an Australian, was adamant, and in the course of argument one
M.P. lost his temper, pulled out his .45, and pointed it at the astonished reporter. Horst Fass, Pulitzer Prize–winning photographer
and Arnett's A.P. colleague, was characteristically professional,
however, and later in the evening, while Barry Zorthian, the U.S.
embassy's chief of public information, was entertaining guests at his
villa, a Vietnamese messenger arrived bearing a large manila enve-
lope. Inside was a glossy black-and-white blowup of an American
M.P. poking his pistol at Peter Arnett, and clipped to the back of
the photograph was Arnett's card. It was the same day that U.S.
spokesmen had denied that orders had been given to get newsmen
off the streets.

But calumny and harassment reflect a reactive, last-ditch defense. The old military adage has it that the best defense is an
offense, and offense in the Information War is the mission of the
Snow Machine. As the United States became more deeply involved
and committed in the Vietnam war and as public opinion in this
country began increasingly to question the validity of that involvement and of the policies that required it, snarling at working reporters, unequipped as they are with the magical contact lenses that
enable one to envision the emperor's clothes on bare-assed royalty,
was obviously not enough. A more positive approach had to be
developed, one that wooed as well as punished. And while the

increasing American buildup necessitated such a development, it also made it easier, for the situation changed drastically as Vietnam became more and more an American war. The relationships between action and image were more in the control of Americans than they could ever have been before. Americans were no longer limited to trying to guide and/or apologize for the South Vietnamese but, on the one hand, exercised far greater control over those actions and, on the other, performed a much greater part of the action themselves. Also, as the American buildup continued, more and more American reporters were sent to Saigon, not so much to cover Vietnam as to cover Americans at war. Both the "pessimism" and the expertise of the old hands was increasingly diluted by the flood of reporters sent to write about U.S. military operations and how home-town Johnny was faring in his fight against the Asian hordes; the more so as the process of attrition— war weariness, homesickness, routine transfer, and casualties— began to thin the ranks of the veteran reporters.

And with the beginning of a large-scale American presence came a Madison Avenue expertise in public-relations gimmickry which few U.S. missions in foreign countries are able to command. South Vietnamese authorities, too, were urged (not always successfully) to upgrade at least their surface attitudes toward the press and to expand and improve facilities for handling newsmen and their needs. After all, American public opinion was as important to the success of the South Vietnamese government's cause as it was to the careers of American professionals in Saigon and politicians in Washington.

In the strictly military area the buildup improved the situation insofar as the quicksand of the complex and intractable political-guerrilla conflict tended to be replaced by a more conventional type of contest, particularly as the North Vietnamese began to match the U.S. presence with the introduction of their own regular units. In several respects it looked like an entirely new ball game, and all previous bets were off. It was, in a sense, a new ball game, but a far more complex one, in fact, and often covered by reporters with no previous experience or background in Asia, not to mention Vietnam, who were therefore much easier to guide or mislead. The

Washington-Saigon Establishment had regained the information initiative. The Snow Machine had now arrived in Vietnam, its parts were assembled, and its work of stamping out the impressions and images officials wanted the American people to receive from Vietnam had begun.

The physical plant of the Vietnam model of the Snow Machine is a modern, air-conditioned building on the corner of Nguyen Hue and Le Loi streets in downtown Saigon, a block away from the two principal residences of foreign newsmen, the Caravelle and Continental hotels, and half a block in another direction from Saigon's City Hall. The building houses the offices of the Joint U.S. Public Affairs Office, or JUSPAO. It is windowless on the ground floor and is entered through either of two doors made of thick bulletproof glass. Occupying its cubicles are representatives from all four major services—the Army, the Navy, the Air Force, and the Marine Corps—plus civilian representatives of the U.S. Agency for International Development and the U.S. Information Agency, whose task it is to feed authorized information to the press, handle (if not answer) questions, and assist newsmen in getting about the country to cover their stories. It is also the central clearinghouse for press accreditation with U.S. forces in Vietnam, Military Assistance Command Vietnam (M.A.C.V.).

In addition to servicing bona-fide newsmen, JUSPAO produces bales of its own product. The building is headquarters to a number of lower-echelon civilian employees whose task it is to cover, as reporters, events and situations which their superiors want publicized; one or more of these is always to be found in the entourage of the junketing politician from the States, no matter how unnewsworthy he and his trip might be. Their material is available free, ordinarily, to anyone who is interested. The military counterparts of these indentured journalists are to be found throughout Vietnam with every major military unit in the country. Their output, too, much of it in the form of unit newspapers, is readily available at the house on Nguyen Hue.

The central event at JUSPAO is the 5 P.M. briefing ("the Five O'Clock Follies") held seven days a week in a small auditorium on the building's ground floor, where reporters who happen to be in town gather to be fed the cabalistic facts and figures of the day's war: operations launched and closed out; the KIA's, WIA's, and MIA's (killed, wounded, and missing in action); bombing raids and sorties; planes lost; the new number of refugees; and the itinerary of the latest visiting fireman. These are provided by three briefers who stand on a stage before five large map boards depicting North Vietnam and the four corps areas of South Vietnam, discernible under a clutter of celluloid numbers, red and blue arrows, and little blue bombs (the numbers refer to items in the daily handout, the red arrows to enemy actions, the blue arrows to U.S. operations, and the little blue bombs to bombing missions). One of the briefers is a civilian, representing the civilian side of the mission and its activities; he is, in fact, the embassy spokesman. The other two report on the military side of the war, one on ground action, the other on air activities. This small, windowless auditorium is not only the focal point of JUSPAO's activities, it is also the principal battleground of the Vietnam Information War.

From the JUSPAO hub the Machine fans out to the various press centers scattered about the country and operated by the U.S. military commands in the areas. The most elaborate of these is the Danang Press Center and Combat Information Bureau, which is run by the Marines. The press centers are miniature repetitions of the JUSPAO function, but adding the provision of bed and board (at a fairly low price) and in some cases a bar as well. At the JUSPAO building in Saigon the correspondent books transportation, (aboard one of several C-130 courier flights that traverse the country daily) to the area he wishes to visit. From the local press center, which he usually makes his headquarters during his stay in the area, he is taken, usually by jeep, truck, or helicopter, to the specific place or unit he wishes to see. Often even the area press centers are duplicated up the line by facilities set up by smaller units from division down to regiment, particularly when the unit is involved in a major operation and is getting, or expects to get, significant press attention. At each of these way stations the correspondent finds officers and men whose job it is to brief him, escort him, guard him, and in addition, men whose job it is to duplicate him—the military reporters whose assignment is to cover the activities of their units and to write stories both for publication in the unit's newspaper and for distribution to correspondents and to newspapers and news services at home. (In the October 10, 1966, issue of *The New Leader* magazine General S. L. A. Marshall wrote, in an article blasting the Saigon press corps, that it was not the duty of the Army "to function as war reporter to the nation." My response to that statement, in a subsequent issue of the magazine, was that the General may have been right, but the number of officers and men the Army employed in that activity might mislead people.)

The functioning of the Machine is far more complex than its structural outline would indicate. Its relationship with the working reporter is a largely benevolent one; its role is one of assistance both in work and in comfort. It does not, however, function primarily to provide information, as a public-information network is supposed to do, but acts principally as an instrument of propaganda. Its efforts are focused on guiding, shaping, and influencing the outflow of news in the interests of Administration policy and the ideas, reputations, and personal careers of those responsible for implementing Washington's policies in Vietnam. And when a lie is required, it lies.

It is not an altogether uniform performance (men in the field, even public-information officers, often couldn't care less about the Information War, being too busy with the other kind, and tend to be fairly frank and outspoken), and it operates within the limitations placed upon it by a democracy, which still demands that it pay more than lip service to the tradition of the free press and to the professional requirements of those who represent the people's right to know. But against these handicaps it has developed a rather high degree of sophistication and a series of techniques that have been considerably refined, by now, through years of application and adjustment.

The Numbers Game

"Write that down," the King said to the jury, and the jury eagerly wrote down all three dates on their slates, and then added them up, and reduced the answer to shillings and pence.
—Lewis Carroll, *Alice in Wonderland*

The abuse of statistics by manipulation to present a desired picture is one of the principal intellectual corruptions of our time, one to which the great majority of Americans, entranced with the achievements and acquirements of science and technology, are most susceptible. The manipulation of statistics for propagandistic purposes was largely pioneered by the advertising industry, but the political and military establishments were not slow in recognizing its potential. And nowhere has the full range of that potential been so thoroughly explored and exploited as in official reporting on the Vietnam war.

In conventional warfare, such as World War II and Korea, military progress is registered in largely topographical terms: miles covered, hills and ridges taken, towns occupied, islands captured, and so forth. In a genuine guerrilla war—that is to say, a political war in which guerrilla forces, in Mao Tse-tung's image, are fish swimming in the sea of the people—topography, or real estate, matters little and proves nothing. The goal here, theoretically and ultimately, is "the hearts and minds" of the people. But that is a vague and insubstantial kind of thing to feed the computers, and so a more manageable concept is used as the chief index of success: the reduction of the enemy's forces. More than just an index, this is also seen by most Americans in Vietnam as the key method of reaching the goal, whatever might be said about "pacification," "revolutionary development," and so on. "Grab 'em by the balls," one high-ranking Marine officer explained the theory, "and their hearts and minds will follow." The way one measures the reduction of enemy forces, of course, is by counting their bodies. From this late contribution to military science has come the institution of the "body-count."

The reduction formula was used with complete success by the British in Malaya, a campaign often cited as the model of how to wage a counterguerrilla war. The guerrillas in the Malayan insurrection, however, were largely Chinese nationals with little or no reenforcement or supply from outside and very limited opportunity for recruitment within Malaya itself, representing as they did a quite distinctive racial minority. Essentially, the Malayan guerrilla forces constituted a distinct maximum quantity that could be, and was, systematically reduced to nothing, or near nothing.

The situation in Vietnam, in all the above respects, was quite different. Nonetheless, the body-count became and remains the single most important index of military success. It was the cornerstone of General William C. Westmoreland's "search-and-destroy" strategy. As a result, the world was introduced to one of the more grisly public-relations performances in recorded history. The progress of every military operation, offensive or defensive, is measured by the number of enemy bodies it accounts for. Thousands of man hours have been expended in the noxious business of digging up enemy bodies after an area has been cleared simply in order to count them. Sometimes they are reburied; often there isn't time.

Naturally enough, pressure for evidence of success—that "coonskin on the wall," as one exalted American liked to call it—and the natural avarice of men and organizations for self-advertisement and advancement led to exaggeration—a veritable policy of exaggeration. This exaggeration took a number of forms, and most of them have become almost routine.

In August of 1966 I joined a Marine battalion, the Second Battalion of the Fourth Marine Regiment, operating just south of the DMZ during Operation Hastings, the first large-scale operation in that area and one of the costliest up to that time. The battalion moved from a hilltop position it had been occupying and, after an hour's march, entered a small valley shaped like a narrow horseshoe. North Vietnamese, invisible in scrub and forest on the far side of the valley, took the unit under fire. The Marines returned the fire with automatic weapons and mortars. For thirty minutes it was all crash and bang; tracers from the machine guns and geysers of smoke and dirt from the mortar rounds were all one could see. When the din eased, I went over to talk with the battalion commander.

"We got thirteen of them," he told me with a straight face.

Incredulous, I asked him how he could tell he got thirteen of anything. The valley was a good two hundred yards across, and there was nothing visible on the other side but bushes and trees.

"That's how many we estimate were there," he replied. "And they aren't shooting anymore, are they?"

I had to admit they were not. But I also had to admit, when I flew back to Dong Ha that evening, that the only casualties I had seen had been two dead Marines and half a dozen wounded ones and that I had not talked to anyone who had seen more. The battalion remained in position for the night and pulled out of the area the next day without making a sweep of the slope on the far side of the valley to count their "kill." But surely enough, the figure "13" was awarded 2/4 on the battle report issued to newsmen in Dong Ha and Danang that night and included in the total figures for the operation released to reporters at the Follies in Saigon.

Two years later, in the aftermath of the 1968 Tet offensive, I ran into the same battalion quite by accident while accompanying a Marine medivac helicopter mission. Although it was the same unit I had been with during Operation Hastings in 1966, its personnel—officers and men—had changed completely, in all probability twice over, since that time. But some things never change. The battalion was engaged in an attack against a well dug-in enemy force in the village of Lam Xuan, situated five miles east of Dong Ha, on the coastal plain of Quang Tri Province. The helicopter crew I was with had been called in for emergency medical evacuation after 2/4 had begun to suffer serious casualties in the action. The lead platoon of one of its companies, Fox, had been cut down as it approached the village across open paddies. Night was closing in. Most of the platoon were dead, including its medical corpsman; wounded men were crying out for help, but no one could get to them. Later that evening and on into the night I sat in the emergency room of the forward hospital at Dong Ha as chopper after chopper arrived to unload casualties from Fox Company and its sister units. Ultimately, most of Fox Company was brought in on them. Many of the remainder lay wounded or dead in the muck of the paddies in front of Lam Xuan. Toward midnight another company advanced in an effort to evacuate what was left of Fox's lead platoon, but they were driven off by a North Vietnamese counterattack, suffering their own casualties. Some of the wounded in the forward paddies, where no one could get to them, died that night where they lay. Not until the following morning, which found the North Vietnamese gone from the village (or what used to be a village), were the remnants of Fox Company, wounded *and* dead, evacuated. But the first report received in Danang and read to reporters there the next day stated that the fight had resulted in one dead and twenty-four wounded Marines, and thirty-two enemy bodies! Even if one assumes it was simply an early report from the point of view of the Marine casualties, somebody was counting the enemy's dead when said enemy was preventing him from getting to and pulling out his own wounded.

I have been told by Marine officers that their units do not add a body to their count "until somebody has put a foot on it." That may be true of some but certainly not of all. The Marines, however, are no worse (and perhaps are even somewhat better) about body-count exaggeration than many Army units. But far from being isolated incidents, such episodes are everyday run-of-the-mill occurrences in Vietnam. Many have been the times when correspondents on the scene of a battle have been at a loss to explain how a particular body-count was arrived at, and equally at a loss to find anyone who could adequately explain it to them. A number of times patrols have been ambushed short of their objective and forced to retreat, leaving some equipment behind; they nevertheless came out with that old body-count—always in considerable excess of their own casualties. Such flagrant excesses are frowned upon in Saigon because they have a tendency to backfire, PR-wise, and discredit the whole body-count concept. But as long as exaggeration and invention are not obvious, they are just part of the game.

One regularly employed technique approaches statistical insanity. When a unit engages the enemy, an estimate of the enemy's strength is attempted—even though he may be (and usually is) invisible in thick jungle or elephant grass—from the volume and nature of fire received. In a fire-fight of any size prodigious amounts of artillery and air support are invariably called in on the enemy positions. When the battle is over and reporting time has come, a *probable* "kill" figure is extrapolated from the *estimated* density of enemy troops hit by a known or approximate number of artillery and mortar rounds, bombs, and rockets. Such abstrusely calculated figures frequently go into the total body-count without a single corpse having been sighted. Helicopter and fighter-bomber pilots daily bring back body-counts, having made a quick count or estimate of black dots still lying on the ground after the bombing and strafing runs.

If the Americans exaggerate, the South Vietnamese fantasize. There is usually some discernible relationship between reality and the figures reported by American units. Not so with the South Vietnamese. Their "body-counts" are so often so absurd that experienced reporters no longer pay any attention to them. American officials know this and laugh about it privately, but they seldom hesitate to include such figures in the country-wide body-count listed in their own daily and weekly reports. This is partly to avoid bruising the sensibilities of their hosts and allies. But one suspects that it is also partly because it looks good in Washington.

There is another facet of this macabre procedure which requires mention; it is one that occurs even when somebody does "put a foot" on the bodies. This is the tendency to count all corpses lying around after a battle as "enemy dead." In populated areas this count not infrequently includes the bodies of people who had nothing more to do with the fighting than their misfortune to be caught in the middle of it. When the battle has been for a fortified guerrilla village, it is all a matter of interpretation: The one usually employed is that everyone in the village was an enemy and now properly belongs in the body-count, including the chickens, goats, and ducks. It has frequently been observed that no one has ever collected reasonable statistics on the number of civilians killed in the Vietnam war. This is not a statistic with which the statisticians in Saigon and Washington are particularly concerned. But even if they were, accurate statistics in this area would not be possible, and never will be, for the very reason that too many dead Vietnamese civilians have already been sucked into the insatiable maw of the "enemy killed" column.

The appalling implications of this practice were laid bare, almost incidentally, in the revelation of the massacre by American troops of "more than one hundred" men, women, and children in the hamlet of Mylai 4 on March 16, 1968. The shocking story caused United Press International to check its files for official press releases on the action handed out at the time. The newsletter of the Americal Division, the parent unit of the soldiers charged with the mass murder, reported it in the following standard manner: "Jungle Warriors (the 11th Light Infantry Brigade) together with artillery and helicopter support hit the village of Mylai early yesterday morning. Contacts throughout the morning and early afternoon resulted in 128 enemy killed, 13 suspects detained, and 3 weapons captured."* *The New York Times* ran essentially the same story on its front page of March 17, 1968. A subsequent edition of the Americal newsletter, published on August 1, 1968, reported that the units involved in the operation had killed a total of 196 "enemy soldiers" in two engagements with a "Vietcong battalion near the village of Mylai."† The facts, as they finally saw light twenty months later, revealed that between 100 and 500 women, children, and old men were gunned down at point-blank range by American soldiers who had herded them into clusters while burning the village and who then proceeded to slaughter them with automatic M-16 fire.

Actually, the body-count itself is only half of the equation used in Vietnam as the chief index of military success. The full equation is known as the kill-ratio, which compares the number of enemy soldiers killed with the number of allied troops killed. A commander doesn't get any points for killing three hundred of the enemy if he loses that many of his own men. In fact, a kill-ratio of less than 10 to 1 is considered a shadowed victory, and this factor often escalates exaggerations of the body-count. One of the longstanding jokes among reporters in Vietnam is that the South Vietnamese, in particular, compute their kill-ratio by dividing the actual number of their own casualties by three to report their own dead and then tripling their actual casualties to arrive at the enemy bodycount. In the past similar A.R.V.N. procedures have been motivated not only by a desire to look good but also by the practice among many Vietnamese commanders of failing to report gaps in the ranks of their units so that they could continue to collect and personally pocket the missing man's pay, be he killed in action or a deserter (this has also been one of the difficulties in computing the real strength of the Vietnamese Army, as well as the number of its

* Quoted in *The New York Times,* November 26, 1969.
† Quoted *ibid.*

deserters). Thus, the flick of a pen in a Saigon office or a field headquarters can transform a grim defeat into the most astonishing of victories, and transform a poor officer into a relatively wealthy man in the bargain.

Another complicating factor in this reporting process is the political impact at home of American casualties. This was especially true in the first weeks of 1968, when American public opinion was reeling under the onslaught of the Tet offensive. Basically, there are two methods of statistical manipulation used to soften that impact. The first, which might be called the dribble method, was employed in the casualty reporting from Lam Xuan. It is quite possible that thirty-four enemy bodies *were* counted when the Marines finally entered the village. But one thing is clear: The full number of American casualties was not given in that first report following the battle. The figure was raised in a subsequent release (and even then it was only a partial tally), but when the story was current, it was one dead and twenty-four wounded.

Given the emphasis of present-day news media on speed and currency, it is invariably the first statement made, the first description cabled, which places an event in the public consciousness and shapes the public's attitude toward it. For an entire story to be late is one thing. For a story to be released in dribbles is quite another. If the story is deemed important enough to be "front-paged," even the most serious revisions, corrections, and additions filed later will go deep in another story or on a far inside page, if they are used at all. Given the time limitations of television news, one can almost forget about revisions and updating, except in the most important of stories. The unfortunate tendency is to highlight what happened today at the expense of yesterday's updating, even when today's event is essentially unimportant. This is doubly true, of course, in periods when a dozen new stories are breaking every day, some of them with undeniable importance. The practice of dribbling out the facts a little at a time accomplished two things in the case of the Lam Xuan story: It greatly reduced the possibility of the battle being given much press attention beyond a couple of lines in a daily–survey–type story, and it established the impression, unlikely to be challenged by later stories given any prominence, that the kill-ratio at Lam Xuan was 32 to 1, when in fact it was almost even. More than any other technique, the use of the "dribble" method demonstrates how sophisticated the Snow Machine's knowledge of its other enemy, the press, has become.

The other manipulative method employed to soften the impact of American casualties can be called submersion. This is a method made possible by the use of adjectives rather than numbers in reporting casualties from specific engagements. Before 1966 the practice of the military in Vietnam had always been to list for individual battles, as well as for country-wide totals, the numbers of wounded and dead suffered by American units. In 1966 the practice was altered: Total figures would be given, but ostensibly to avoid giving the enemy information, aid, and comfort, losses in particular battles would be listed only as "light," "moderate," or "heavy." This practice was so abused, however (as might have been predicted), and so escalated the skepticism with which the press received official reports that M.A.C.V., in the interests of its own credibility, chose to resume reporting the specific numbers again. Then, during the 1968 Tet offensive, there was a partial return to the use of adjectives (which is still in force), this with respect to enemy attacks on fixed installations. The purpose of this change was, indeed, one of security, of denying the enemy useful military information.

The story cited as the prime example of the reason for this policy involved, ironically, not the civilian newsmen but the Armed Forces Radio-Television Service. A.F.R.T.S., which broadcasts music, military homilies, lugubrious prayers by chaplains, and a highly circumspect and censored news program to American troops in Vietnam, had, it seems, been broadcasting live, or nearly so, from a U.S. base under rocket attack. In the course of the broadcast the announcer was describing the incoming rounds, telling where they hit and how much damage they were doing, and "acting for all the world," said one horrified military spokesman, "like an infiltrated North Vietnamese forward observer. If Charlie out there had himself a transistor radio, all he had to do was listen to A.F.R.T.S. to adjust his fire!"

Most reporters understood the restriction as a military necessity and took no offense from it. The adjectives were back in use, however, and were once again available for abuse.

"Light" means that a unit's casualties have not significantly impaired its effectiveness. "Moderate" casualties mean that the unit's effectiveness has been reduced but not ended. "Heavy" casualties mean anything from "rendered militarily ineffective" to wiped out. There are no reliable percentile equivalents of these terms that I am aware of, but most reporters, from experience, read "light" to mean casualties under 10 per cent, "moderate," from 10 to 30 per cent, and "heavy," anything from 30 to 100 per cent. There being no real definitions or official equivalents, however, the characterization of casualties is entirely up to the unit commanders and their superiors, and one person's "heavy" is easily another's "moderate."

The submersion method does not rely wholly on the inexactitude of the adjectives; much more important is the manipulation of the reporting units. If a company suffers 50 per cent wounded and dead, its casualties, by anyone's standards, have been heavy. They have been, that is, if the company itself is the reporting unit. If the battalion is used as the reporting unit, the same number of casualties represents only a 12½ per cent loss. If the regiment is used as the reporting unit, the same number of casualties hardly shows on the chart, and so on. Thus a "heavy" disaster for any given unit can be reported in terms of "light" to "moderate" casualties by the simple expediency of submerging its casualties in the report of a larger unit. This has been done many times in Vietnam, where operations involving battalions and even brigades climax in a fire-fight limited to the front of a single company.

The most flagrant, large-scale example of this kind of statistical manipulation in my own experience was the post-battle report by the Marines on the fight for the city of Hue during the months of February and March, 1968. By far the lion's share of the fighting in that city was done by a single battalion, the First Battalion of the Fifth Marines. That battalion suffered—in one of the bitterest, bloodiest battles of the entire war—what must by any standards be described as "heavy" casualties. Day after day, inch by inch, house by house, they advanced through the old walled section of the city where the enemy had his greatest strength, and they paid a high price for every block. Weather conditions sided with the enemy: The only entrance and exit for most of the battle was by helicopter, but low cloud-ceilings curtailed replacement of both casualties and supplies. At times it was not even possible to get the wounded out. Inevitably, the number of effectives in the battalion fell progressively; at one point the unit was below half strength, and some of its companies were down to quarter strength and even lower. Several times Navy convoys attempted to get through to the Marines of 1/5 via the Perfume River, which separates the new section of Hue on the south bank (already secured) from the old Imperial City, or Citadel, on the north bank, where the fighting raged for nearly a month. Each time, until the last few days of the battle, the convoys were turned back by heavy and accurate mortar, rocket, and recoilless-rifle fire from the North Vietnamese entrenched along the walls of the Citadel. Until the battle for the old city was over, 1/5 was never relieved, though it had become, in the parlance, "militarily ineffective." It was, however, reenforced in the last three days of the battle by two companies from a sister battalion. When the reenforcements arrived, they outnumbered the effectives still left in 1/5.

When it was all over, the Marines issued a press release stating that the fighting for the city of Hue had resulted in only "light" casualties for our side. Included in the report were *all* Marine ground units in the general area, some of which had been only temporarily involved in the month-long battle, others only marginally involved, and still others not at all. Further, the figures did *not* include the casualties suffered by the Navy convoys that tried to break the North Vietnamese ring around the city, nor the helicopter crewmen killed and wounded in the effort to supply the Marines in the Citadel, nor the casualties of the First Cavalry (Air Mobile) units that played a key part in the final recapture, moving in on the city from the north against resistance so stiff they were repulsed on two occasions. No composite figures on the casualties suffered in the *actual* battle for Hue were, to my knowledge, ever issued. Not only were 1/5's casualties submerged in most of the entire Marine force in Vietnam, but conversely, the total casualties in the battle were fragmented on the basis of separate services. The Marines being the service principally involved in the fight, theirs were the casualties identified with it; and theirs, by the process of submersion, were "light." Needless to say, the political impact at home of "light casualties" is predictably softer than the numerical produce of the meat-grinder through which the First Battalion of the Fifth Marines was fed.

Another key aspect of the numbers game involves the amount of territory and the percentage of population alleged to be, at any given time, under Government (South Vietnamese) control. These figures have been generally as unreliable as the body-count and the kill-ratio, but they are key indexes, far more significant than the absolute *or* relative number of casualties inflicted. The standards used to measure Government control are questionable at best. Generally, "Government control" means Government presence—a highly tenuous identification, as the Vietcong have been known to exert real control in hamlets and villages actually occupied by Government troops. Frequently, the term means even less. Government control has been claimed for areas in which Government troops could move in large numbers in daytime, though they could not do so in smaller numbers nor at night in any numbers. I shall never forget a visit in 1966 to a province capital near Saigon, where an American adviser showed me a map on which most of the province area was shaded blue—meaning Government-controlled. After we discussed the local situation, during which I explained what I wanted to do and see while in the area, the officer bit his lip and brought me back to the map. He then circumscribed a small circle within the blue area, tightly drawn around the capital city, where he said it was safe to go in the daytime, providing I had an armed escort with me.

There are three categories used in determining the degree of Government control of areas in Vietnam: (1) Government-controlled areas, (2) contested areas, and (3) Vietcong-controlled areas. What makes statistics in this realm so unreliable is that the Government (and the Americans) often insists that areas genuinely controlled by the National Liberation Front are contested areas (meaning that Government or U.S. patrols and/or search-and-destroy operations occasionally penetrate them) and that areas genuinely contested are Government-controlled.

But surely the most cynical ploy in the numbers game is the refugee count. At least until the 1968 Tet offensive, when their very numbers became an indication of the enemy's success in dislocating the most "secure" areas of the country, refugees were counted like money in the bank by the Americans and their Vietnamese allies; refugees were proof that an increasing number of Vietnamese preferred our brand to the competition. The people were, supposedly, "voting with their feet," just about the best propaganda anybody can ask for. But away from the press briefings in the air-conditioned rooms of military and civilian planners those numbers served as an index of the progress of a major strategy in the Vietnam war, one that has received all too little attention.

Ask most literate, newspaper-reading Americans what the basic *military* strategy of the United States in Vietnam is, and they will probably respond with some version of "search and destroy," which is, indeed, the basic concept employed by American and allied forces vis-à-vis Vietcong and North Vietnamese units themselves. But this is only one part of a strategy developed over the years of American involvement in the Vietnam struggle. If, as Mao stated, the guerrilla is a fish swimming in the sea of the people, then one solution to the problem, from the antiguerrilla or counterinsurgency point of view held by Americans in Vietnam, is to drain the sea. Actually, there are *two* seas in which the Vietnamese guerrilla swims. One is indeed the people; the other is the thick double- and triple-canopied jungle that covers much of the country. The drainage of the latter sea is primarily accomplished through defoliation, the systematic poisoning of vegetation in areas known or believed to be used as sanctuaries by the guerrillas; it is done by spraying the jungle with herbicides from the air. The code name given the process, an irony with a special Texas flavor, is Operation Ranchhand. Defoliation is also visited on crop-growing areas where it is believed the guerrillas get, or might get, their food supply. By the end of 1967 an estimated 5 per cent of all land under cultivation had been so treated. Defoliation of crop land has the added advantage of aiding in the drainage of that other sea, the people.

In 1966 the chief tactic used to drain the people sea was the old carrot-and-stick approach. Villagers in areas held by or easily accessible to the Vietcong were warned to leave their homes and come into Government-secured areas or risk being bombed. The warnings were usually given by means of leaflet drops and loudspeaker harangues from circling aircraft and were frequently followed up by bombing missions in the general area, even when no significant *enemy* targets (that is to say, concentrated enemy units) were known to be in the target areas. The bombs were exclamation points for the leaflets. That was the stick. The carrot was the promise of food at refugee centers and the payment of a small sum of money—though not so small to the peasant farmer. Sometimes the tactic worked and sometimes it didn't. But even when it did work, the results were often of questionable value. One of the major problems turned out to be that people would bring leaflets into the Government refugee centers, eat a meal or two, collect their reward, and slip away to return to their own Vietcong-infested areas. Subsequently, a sterner but more effective method was employed: the removal of an entire hamlet's residents by force, after which the whole place would be obliterated, leaving nothing to return to—a process eloquently chronicled in Jonathan Schell's *The Village of Ben Suc.** But still the refugees so garnered were said to be, like those who came south from North Vietnam in 1954, "voting with their feet" against Communist terror and oppression and were duly entered in the totals computed and issued in Saigon.

Words and Phrases

"When I *use a word," Humpty Dumpty said in a rather scornful tone, "it means just what I choose it to mean—neither more nor less."*

"The question is," said Alice, "whether you can *make words mean different things."*

"The question is," said Humpty Dumpty, "which is to be master —that's all."

—Lewis Carroll, *Alice in Wonderland*

* New York: Alfred A. Knopf, Inc., 1967.

Inextricably enmeshed with statistical manipulation is the manipulation of words and concepts to project a desired image often
contrary to fact; both the kill-ratio and the refugee count are prime
examples of how the two methods work together to achieve a single
effect. When Admiral Felt called Ap Bac a "victory" for South
Vietnamese forces, he did so on the basis of the fact that "we took
the village," an assertion temporarily true in the most narrow and
technical sense but one that grotesquely distorted reality. The
attempt was to place an entirely irrelevant concept, like a cosmetic
shroud, over a bitter reality. The exploitation of refugees for
propaganda is a similar exercise. And in the simple task of trying to
soften or mask the undeniably brutal realities of the war nothing
works quite so well as the kind of technical euphemism which
removes the flesh and blood of humanity from the picture and
substitutes graphs, charts, and the dehumanized and dehumanizing
syntax and vocabulary of the military: "Recon by fire," "free strike
zones," and "enemy structures" are three widely used examples in a
long list.

"Recon by fire" is a military term that quite explicitly describes a
standard tactical operation in which an advancing unit accom-
plishes its reconaissance of an area where the enemy is suspected to
be hiding by firing into it. The assumption is that the enemy will
realize he is discovered and will fire back or flee if he is not already
dead or wounded. In Vietnam, however, the tactic is often employed against villages, and its likely effect on civilians in the
villages is obvious. In these cases even such standard terms as "VC"
and "enemy" become euphemistic. If it is, indeed, a Vietcong
village, even noncombatant women and children are so classified;
there are no "civilians" in a Vietcong village. The fact that this has
a certain amount of truth in it, that a number of women and
children in such villages are frequently found fighting alongside the
men, is often cited as an excuse. But to the GI participating in the
fight it is more than an excuse; it seems ample reason. German
troops advancing across Russia and France must have reasoned in
a very similar manner.

"Free strike zones" and "free fire zones" are areas considered
Vietcong-controlled and where no civilians, unless they are Viet-

cong, are supposed to be. They are so designated to allow planes and artillery to strike at will any "target" sighted. They also function as dumping grounds on which bombers can unload any unused bombs or rockets on their return to base. Woe betide anything or anyone that moves in such an area and is sighted by an artillery observer or a forward air controller—be it Vietcong, a group of mountain tribesmen, or a herd of water buffalo.

"Enemy structures" may be bunkers, or (in North Vietnam) they may be barracks and warehouses, or they may be the huts of a village. All are listed in the daily handouts in Saigon under the general euphemism "enemy structures," like the "body-counts" computed from the air. Like most such terms, these are not simply phrases for public consumption; they are the language of the military, and the pilots and troops not only speak with them but also think with them. They constitute the techno-bureaucratic method of euphemising and depersonalizing the daily details of warfare, which is what the "word game" is all about. Similarly, when Harrison Salisbury, of *The New York Times,* went to Hanoi and reported that North Vietnam had been suffering significant civilian casualties from the American bombing ("enemy structures" were claimed to be the sole targets), a number of U.S. pilots who had taken part in those raids disputed his findings. One of them was Navy Commander Robert C. Mandeville, who had been commanding officer of VA-65, a squadron of Intruder jet bombers. An interview on the subject with Commander Mandeville was printed in the Norfolk (Virginia) *Ledger-Star* of Wednesday, December 28, 1966. Later, in a telephone interview with the Commander, the *Times* extracted one of the more memorable quotes of the war. "He's describing what he's seen on the ground," Mandeville told the *Times.* "I guess we're looking at it from different points of view."

"Winning hearts and minds" is surely the greatest clinker of them all. As indicated before, the phrase describes for the most part what is essentially a contest of terrors—with each side trying to prove to the general populace that they are not safe with the other. For instance, in the belief of many Americans in Vietnam, the negative political effects of South Vietnamese civilian casualties

caused by U.S. bombs and shells is more than offset by the proven
fact that people tend to go where the least danger is and to obey the
man with the biggest stick, regardless of their feelings about him.
This is also the main thrust of a rather more honestly named
program, pacification.

The corruption of language, of vision, and of sensibility which
has risen like a poisonous ground fog from the Vietnam war sometimes produces its own parody. Probably the most well known was
the explanation for the leveling of Ben Tre during the 1968 Tet
offensive. It had to be destroyed, an American officer told reporters, in order to save it. Indeed, much of South Vietnam has
been experiencing the systematic application of such salvation
techniques for years. "This," wrote former Marine Colonel William
R. Corson, "is the language of madness."*

Jonathan Schell's second Vietnam book, *The Military Half: An
Account of Destruction*† (like *The Village of Ben Suc,* it was
originally a *New Yorker* article), chronicled the "pacification" program in the provinces of Quang Ngai and Quang Tin. It was a
program that involved the wholesale destruction of villages not considered sufficiently under Government or American control (which
was most of both provinces) and the removal of their inhabitants
to crowded, ill-equipped refugee centers. Schell reported that in
1967, 70 per cent of the villages in Quang Ngai Province had
been so destroyed and that as much as 80 per cent of the population lived either in refugee camps or in caves and bunkers beneath
their destroyed homes. Quang Ngai is the province where the hamlet of Mylai 4 is located.‡ Responding to the uproar over the
March, 1968, incident at Mylai, Schell wrote in a letter to *The
New York Times* (November 26, 1969) that at one point the
camps simply became too full, and the Army was told not to bring
any more in. Search-and-destroy operations, however, continued:

* William R. Corson, *The Betrayal* (New York: W. W. Norton & Company,
Inc., 1968), p. 289.
 † New York: Alfred A. Knopf, Inc., 1968.
 ‡ In Vietnam a village is an administrative unit or area composed of any number
of smaller hamlets. Mylai 4, as the numeral indicates, is one of four hamlets with
the same name in the *village* of Songmy, in Quang Ngai Province. The district in
which the village is located is Sontinh.

Only now peasants were not warned before an air-strike was called in on their village. They were killed in their villages because there was no room for them in the swamped pacification camps. . . . Every civilian on the ground was assumed to be enemy by the pilots by nature of living in Quang Ngai, which was largely a free-fire zone. . . . Air-strikes on civilians became a matter of routine. It was under these circumstances of official acquiescence to the destruction of the countryside and its people that the massacre of Songmy occurred.

Concluding his letter, Schell put his finger on what this reporter considers the essence of the Vietnam dilemma and the moral agony it has caused the nation: "Such atrocities were and are the logical consequences of a war directed against an enemy indistinguishable from the people."

In a statement made presenting the President's views on October 26, two weeks after the Songmy story had broken in the press, White House press secretary Ronald L. Ziegler cautioned that "this incident should not be allowed to reflect on the some million and a quarter young Americans who have now returned to the United States after having served in Vietnam with great courage and distinction." I am afraid, however, that it must do just that, just as the low-keyed and frequently defensive public reaction to it must reflect upon the nation as a whole. Nor is it, though certainly the most egregious revealed to date, an isolated incident in the Vietnam war, as many insist. As Schell and others have suggested, it is part of the fabric of that war; its emotional roots are common to Americans serving in Vietnam, particularly in combat positions, even though they may avoid physical implication in such an act; and it proceeds with brutal logic from the twin policies of "search and destroy" and "pacification." Other senseless American atrocities have seen the light of public print in recent months, including the torture-murder of a group of South Vietnamese farmers (*Look* magazine) and Daniel Lang's harrowing tale, "Casualties of War" (*The New Yorker*), which detailed the premeditated kidnapping, prolonged gang-rape, and murder of a young South Vietnamese woman by an American squad on patrol. In none of these cases

are we dealing with individual men, but with units, sometimes acting under orders.

In the case of the murder reported by Lang, the guilty men received courts-martial only after one member of the squad who had
refused to participate, even though his life had been threatened
(his sergeant warned him that if he did not participate, he would
become a "friendly casualty"—even the most depraved speak and
think in techno-military euphemisms), went from one superior
officer after another to report the incident, only to be warned at
each level to forget the matter for his own good. The soldier
finally sought out a more sympathetic chaplain in another unit.
Given a pseudonym by Lang for his protection ("Sven Eriksson"),
he still lives in some fear of his life—though he has been out of
the Army for some months—because his former comrades, who
were given astonishingly short sentences that are regularly short-
ened, will soon be out of prison and may seek revenge.

"Eriksson's" attempts to report what he witnessed may be instructive to those who wonder how the military in Vietnam could keep
the wraps on the Songmy incident for so long. The incident at
Hill 192 (the Lang story) and the incident at Songmy were each
exposed by one man—the former by "Sven Eriksson," acting at
serious peril to his life, the latter by Ronald Ridenhour, a dis-
charged Vietnam veteran who put together the story from recol-
lections of a number of men who had participated in the action or
who had witnessed it. In both cases participants were told by superior officers to keep their mouths shut about it. How many other
incidents of a similar nature have occurred that lack a voice of
conscience, that have not had their Ridenhour or their "Eriksson"?
Songmy was not just a terrible aberration; it is in the nature of
the Vietnam war, the contest of terrors.

One of the participants in the Songmy affair stated that rumors
went through the company afterward that Westmoreland had
learned of the action and that something was afoot from that
quarter (after all, a helicopter pilot who witnessed the massacre
from the air was so appalled that he landed and tried to stop it
after radioing to headquarters—and apparently was responsible for

saving about 150 who had not yet been shot).* The soldier said that subsequently, however, the thing had been shelved, because the South Vietnamese officials in the area were quite delighted about the elimination of this pocket of Vietcong sympathizers and were going to make no trouble. Indeed, when press exposure made the affair a public issue in the United States, an investigation conducted for the South Vietnamese Government by Major General Hoang Xuan Lam, the South Vietnamese commander of I Corps, the area in which Songmy is located, resulted in a Government statement that denied any massacre had taken place and affirmed instead that any civilian deaths in the area were attributable to the Vietcong —even as participants in the action were testifying in the American press. General Lam, it should be noted, went on an inspection tour of ravaged districts in Quang Ngai Province early in 1967. Looking at a scene of almost universal destruction, he is reported to have remarked: "Good! Good! They are all VC. Kill them!"†

On the policy level it is implicitly assumed that this is and always has been a civil war even while official statements for public consumption, both in Saigon and in Washington, deny it and insist on "aggression from the North." Even after the war the South Vietnamese Government must control the population in order to have "won." It must deprive the other side of a base for recruitment, supply, and political support; it must drain Mao's "sea." If this can be done by the wholesale uprooting of village populations and their removal to more secure areas, fine. If not. . . . Actually, many South Vietnamese military men worry about the first alternative creating a political Trojan horse in already secured areas. Those South Vietnamese villagers already infected with the insurgents' virus are less surely and effectively neutralized by relocation than when, to use another famous euphemism to come out of the Vietnam war, "terminated with extreme prejudice." Americans tend to be somewhat less sanguine in this respect, but the theory is not altogether unknown to them. At the level of the individual American soldier the attitude sifts down to the feeling that the enemy is simply the Vietnamese, unless they happen to be wearing the uni-

* *The New York Times,* November 27, 1969.
† Major General Hoang Xuan Lam, quoted by Schell, *The Military Half,* p. 27.

form of the South Vietnamese Army (and, emotionally, sometimes even then).

At a hospital unit at Dong Ha one day in March, 1968 (at about the same time the Songmy incident took place), a young Navy corpsman expressed to me an attitude all too prevalent among Americans in Vietnam. The unit, Delta Medical Company, had earlier been issued orders prohibiting it from administering anything but *initial* emergency treatment to Vietnamese civilians and specifically prohibiting the use of the unit's two operating rooms to treat them. Though the doctors sometimes ignored the order, it was generally adhered to. The subject of the conversation was a four-year-old Vietnamese boy who had fragments from a mine in his head, his chest, his stomach, and his legs. His condition had been stabilized, but he would have to undergo a dangerously bumpy thirty-minute ambulance ride from Dong Ha to the Vietnamese civilian hospital in Quang Tri before he could receive surgery. The corpsman, a kid of no more than twenty, replied with a blasé shrug of his shoulders when I expressed concern that the child might die on the trip to the Quang Tri hospital, which was, in any case, a medical nightmare out of the eighteenth century. "What the hell," he said, "if the kid lives, he'll just grow up to kill more Americans."

Among the more popular examples of the black humor generated by Americans in Vietnam have been variations on the parking-lot theme, *i.e.,* we ought to raze the whole place, pave it over with asphalt, and turn it into a parking lot. (An older, more humane and good-natured favorite was largely gone from the scene after 1965—that of American advisers which went something like: "If we were just advising Charlie instead of the A.R.V.N., we *would* be home by Christmas.") More brutally to the point was the opinion of another young American soldier, an infantryman with the 1st Infantry Division in 1966, who was quoted in John Sack's excellent book, *M,* as having said, "I'd like to burn the whole country down and start again with Americans."*

---

* Quoted by John Sack, *M* (New York: New American Library, Inc., 1967), p. 189.

■ CHAPTER 5 ■

Khe Sanh

The story of Khe Sanh is the most dramatic example since Ap Bac of the discrepancy between the information given out by officials and the observations of newsmen. It is also an excellent example of the manner in which the astigmatism of these officials and their susceptibility to their own propaganda mislead not only the public awareness but also their own policy formulation.

Khe Sanh was originally nothing more than a village in the northwestern corner of South Vietnam about six miles from the Laotian border and eighteen miles south of the Demilitarized Zone. The U.S. Special Forces established their presence in the area very early, both at Khe Sanh itself and at Lang Vei, only two miles from the Laos border. They were there for two reasons: The area was the center of a large concentration of montagnards (mountain tribesmen) of the Bru tribe, whom the Americans recruited as mercenaries to fight the enemy, and the sites straddled two important North Vietnamese infiltration routes into the South—one from Laos along Route 9, a road built by the French, ran from Savannakhet, in western Laos, through Lang Vei, Khe Sanh, and on to the South China Sea in South Vietnam; the other route ran down through the DMZ in the vicinity of Khe Sanh. When Robert McNamara bought the quixotic idea of an electronic barrier across the northern border of South Vietnam, Khe Sanh was assigned the western anchor of that line, and the Marines began to move in. By the end of 1967 the barrier idea had been almost completely abandoned in Washington (military authorities in Vietnam had never favored it), but by then Khe Sanh had become a political issue.

It appears, at least from hindsight, that Khe Sanh was envisioned by the North Vietnamese as the first step in the 1968 Tet offensive. Their buildup in the region in December, 1967, and early January, 1968, was responded to with the hurried reenforcement of a relatively small Marine garrison in the village and around the airstrip by the entire 26th Marine Regiment, a force of some five thousand men, plus a detachment of Navy Seabees, Air Force ground personnel, and a battalion of South Vietnamese Rangers—making a total force of nearly seven thousand. Estimates of the North Vietnamese force were placed at upwards of forty thousand at full tide. General Vo Nguyen Giap, the victor of Dien Bien Phu, vowed to repeat the lesson he had given the French in 1954 for the Americans in 1968—at Khe Sanh. The Americans, in another of those oft-heard (and frequently rued) phrases, expressed delight that their enemy might finally "stand and fight" and confidence that in such a "set-piece" battle they could break the back of the North Vietnamese Army.

The end of 1967 was filled with expressions of great optimism on the part of American officials, civilian and military. Everyone, it seemed, was seeing that "light at the end of the tunnel" glimpsed earlier by Secretary of Defense McNamara. Ironically, this most famous of all last words had been introduced much earlier. More than a decade before, Lieutenant General Henri Navarre, Commandant of French forces in Indochina, had explained the purpose of Dien Bien Phu in identical terms and between the first French paratroop assault on November 21, 1953, and the fall of the garrison on May 7, 1954, he had committed seventeen thousand French troops to a battle that proved to be France's Stalingrad in Southeast Asia. Navarre was quoted by *Time* magazine at the time as having said, "A year ago, none of us could see victory. . . . Now we can see it clearly—*like a light at the end of a tunnel* [my italics]." Even the rhetoric of Khe Sanh was becoming ominous.

There were other similarities. The French had initially gone into Dien Bien Phu to block Vietminh access to Laos, just as the

Marines and Army Special Forces had garrisoned Khe Sanh to block, or at least to monitor, North Vietnamese infiltration (ironically, via Laos) into South Vietnam. Khe Sanh, like Dien Bien Phu, was essentially a valley position centered on an airstrip and ringed by high jungle-covered hills, most of which were held by the enemy. Also, whatever the specific *military* importance of the battle for Dien Bien Phu (even though its forces there represented the cream of the French Army in Indochina), its overriding significance quickly became its political potential. France might well have fought on in Vietnam for quite some time, but the effect of that defeat on the French electorate and National Assembly resulted in almost immediate French capitulation at Geneva. The same political importance quickly became attached to Khe Sanh as dissent against the war grew prodigiously at home. Against the similarities there were, of course, significant differences. The most important of these was the amount of air- and fire-power accessible to the defenders of Khe Sanh, even when under siege—a difference on which the Americans counted everything.

With the increasing North Vietnamese buildup around Khe Sanh and the base's consequent vulnerability, a good deal of nervousness began to emerge among Americans familiar with the situation, even among military officers in Vietnam. Some members of Lieutenant General Robert E. Cushman's staff (the Commandant of Marines in Vietnam at the time), although publicly unanimous in their confidence that Khe Sanh could and should be held, were privately anything but sanguine about the advisability of the venture. President Johnson was so nervous about it himself that he took the unprecedented step of requiring the Joint Chiefs of Staff to sign a letter guaranteeing the successful defense of the base (who said the buck stops here?). At one point during the siege General Westmoreland hedged his bet by admitting that the North Vietnamese might be able to overrun Khe Sanh, but he assured the nervous that the enemy would not be able to hold their prize against an allied counterattack and that their losses would be crippling. Such statements and gestures as these, plus the well-known fact that General Giap had never proved stingy with the expenditure of men when the occasion seemed important enough, made the Marines at Khe

Sanh feel like worms on a fishhook, which is about what they were.

By the time the 1968 Tet offensive got rolling during the first few days of February the siege was complete: Khe Sanh was encircled, access by road had been completely cut, and the nearby Special Forces camp at Lang Vei had been overrun in a battle that saw the first employment by the enemy of tanks in the Vietnamese war. The weather through much of the daytime limited close air support, and enemy approach trenches began to snake slowly toward the Marine perimeter. At a press conference in Danang in late February General Cushman admitted he had begun to read the works of his rival, General Giap (a French reporter remarked in an aside that the General's research was perhaps a bit belated). The ring grew tighter; in the first days of March the airstrip was closed. It had been decided in February that the big four-engine C-130, the cargo workhorse in Vietnam, was too vulnerable to enemy gunners in the surrounding hills—its glide-path was too long. Thereafter, only the smaller C-123, a two-engine version of the C-130, was able to land and take off on the 3,500 foot runway—and only briefly thereafter. Damage to and losses of these planes occurred with dismaying regularity, too, and after North Vietnamese gunners downed an incoming C-123 with forty-five passengers aboard, the airstrip at Khe Sanh was closed to all fixed-wing aircraft. Now all entrance to and exit from Khe Sanh had to be made via helicopter, and re-supply had to be accomplished by means of helicopters and para-chute drops.

By now Khe Sanh, like Dien Bien Phu, had become an issue of the very greatest political magnitude. The justification of Khe Sanh as an outpost blocking North Vietnamese infiltration from the north and west was wearing increasingly thin as reporters who visited Khe Sanh observed that the base was threatened most strongly by enemy forces from the south and east. It was a little like sinking a post in the middle of a river and calling it a dam: The test of a dam is whether or not the flow of water is stopped—and downstream from Khe Sanh was all water. The other justification for Khe Sanh, its use as a "reef" against which the enemy would smash himself, was never borne out, because Giap never launched his attack.

The official U.S. explanations for the failure of the North Vietnamese to attack Khe Sanh were that American airpower had prevented them from getting sufficiently organized and supplied to mount an attack before the cloud-cover of the rainy season ended and that the damage done to their forces by that airpower (which dropped an almost unbelievable tonnage of bombs around Khe Sanh) had crippled their strike potential. Even without the attack, this thesis went, the "reef" concept had been a partial success. What is more, the United States had been saved from a devastating political and psychological defeat.

But this was defining the name of the game after it has already been played and declaring yourself the winner. Much was made of the breakthrough to Khe Sanh by a U.S. task force which technically ended the siege and the base's isolation from the rest of the country. That the breakthrough occurred with only light opposition from the enemy was cited as evidence of the damage that had been done him. It remained for reporters to inform the public that the operation was launched only because intelligence had discovered that the enemy had pulled most of his forces out of the area separating the besieged forces and their rescuers. The siege was not broken; it was abandoned by the enemy. Perhaps he did so because of heavy casualties due to air-strikes; certainly he must have suffered heavily under the pounding. But the results of bombing, however heavy, have generally been considerably less than those claimed for it by military officials—particularly in Vietnam—and there are other explanations more consistent with the facts of the situation.

To begin with, the pressure around Khe Sanh began to ease and ebb away as it became obvious that the Tet offensive had been concluded—or had run out of steam, however one wished to characterize it. Secondly, there are some indications that beyond drawing a steel ring around the base and sending occasional battalion-sized probes against its outposts and perimeter, no serious effort at overrunning the Marines was planned. After the siege was lifted, Colonel David E. Lownds, Khe Sanh's commander, inspected the formerly formidable-looking enemy approach trenches and found them not very impressive after all. They were narrow

and shallow, less than two feet deep, and would require even the
characteristically small Vietnamese to crawl on their stomachs one
at a time—not a very efficient way of getting the large numbers of
men required to make an assault across a denuded no-man's-land
swept by automatic-weapons fire and zeroed in on by artillery and
mortars. Indeed, the trenches looked like they were made more for
show than for use.

The obvious question, then, is what *were* the North Vietnamese
after at Khe Sanh? One way to answer it is to inventory what they
got. Such an inventory was suggested by *The New York Times*
during the first week of the Tet offensive, and it remains in my mind
the best explanation available. In a summary article on the deteriorating situation the *Times* began by observing that the attack on the
cities of South Vietnam came "at a moment when all eyes were
fixed on Khesanh" and continued:

> In the past several months much of the strength of the
> American units that had ringed Saigon for nearly two years had
> been shifted northward to fight North Vietnamese regulars on
> the Cambodian border. . . . The same movement from the
> population centers took place in the central highlands and in the
> northern provinces.
>
> Just the week before last at least 15,000 American troops
> were moved north as reserves for the 5,000 marines isolated at
> Khesanh. . . . It was here, the American command had em-
> phasized, that the major enemy blow had been expected to fall.
> . . . Only time will tell whether what was apparently a well-
> advertised movement by two North Vietnamese divisions into
> the hills around Khesanh was a diversion.

During much of the agonizing month-long battle for the city of
Hue the Americans simply could not summon enough forces to do
the job. For much of the battle there were not enough troops
available to clear the highway between the Marine supply base at
Phu Bai and the city, a road repeatedly closed by North Vietnamese ambushes. Nor were there sufficient forces to close off all
the avenues of reenforcement and resupply for the North Vietnamese holed up in the Citadel. The forces that *were* rushed to Hue

as well as to cities all over the country, either to prevent their capture or to recapture them, denuded the countryside in areas long considered Government-controlled, turning them over to the Vietcong almost by default. In the course of a week the pacification progress of two years went down the drain while "all eyes were fixed on Khesanh" and twenty thousand (more than a full division) of the best troops in the country were tied down in the remote northwestern corner, waiting for a blow that never fell.

With respect to the operation of the Snow Machine, not only Khe Sanh but the entire Tet offensive of 1968 was highly significant: Both demonstrated conclusively that the official story being told the public about conditions in Vietnam was woefully out of touch with reality. As dissent with and repudiation of the Administration's Vietnam policy grew stronger in the United States, Washington ordered greater efforts on the part of the Snow Machine; more ammunition was ordered from Saigon (for this is a reverse war— the guns as well as the logistical flow are turned inward). A strong light was thrown on this phenomenon by Ward Just, the Washington *Post*'s Vietnam correspondent, when he wrote in the November 19, 1967, issue of that paper:

> Quantify us some hearts and minds, the Administration has in effect told its agents in Saigon, or lacking that, give us a measure of how the war is being won. Because if the American people are not convinced that the war is being won, dissent will grow, the polls will plunge and the public demand to disengage would become irresistible.
>
> There were "hundreds of cables," according to an official who should know, between Washington and Saigon requesting answers on just this point. . . . Saigon responded, and there is now a statistical deluge. . . . The statistics are familiar: the favorable kill-ratio; the favorable weapons-loss ratio; the decline in Communist-initiated attacks; a decline in South Vietnamese army desertions—and now the first reliable index of population control, the so-called HES, or Hamlet Evaluation System. . . . But most officials believe the crux to be not *control* of the population by Saigon but the allegiance of the population to Saigon. Beyond that, there is the difficulty of assessing whether or not

a hamlet is secure only because of the presence of American troops. . . . What will happen, one official wondered, if a year from now we have, say, 85% of the Vietnamese people under Saigon control and the war has not abated and American casualties remain about the same?

The official quoted by Just scarcely had to wait a year, as events even at that time might have indicated. In any case, he was expressing a nervousness felt by many individual Americans in Vietnam about the operation of the Machine and the corruption of policy-making which that operation entails.

A demonstration of Saigon's response to Washington's urgent demands for home-front propaganda ammunition is dramatically available from the pages of *The New York Times* in its reporting of officials' statements on "how the war is being won" in the fall of 1967:

November 16: "WAR GAINS CALLED VERY ENCOURAGING BY WESTMORELAND: Never More Heartened in His 4 Years in Vietnam, Commander Declares; HOME FOR TOP REVIEW: [*now the truth*] General Asserts He Wants Promised Reinforcements As Soon As Possible."

November 22: "WAR OF ATTRITION CALLED EFFECTIVE BY WESTMORELAND: He and Bunker Foresee a Reduction in U.S. Role If Progress Continues":

> Their conclusion is that the United States and its allies are steadily wearing down the enemy at the present level of force and supply on both sides, and their assumption is that the Soviet Union, China and the rest of the Communist world will not provide the additional weapons and men necessary to restore the military balance that is now going against Hanoi and the Vietcong.

And in the same issue there is this fascinating piece of information:

> They are privately critical of past U.S. intelligence estimates made by an American officer who has been transferred to an-

other post, and confident about the intelligence estimates they are now getting from his replacement.

This part of the story, told in James Reston's column, did not specify whether Westmoreland and Bunker were critical of the former intelligence officer because his estimates were overoptimistic or too pessimistic. In either case, the events of the coming February proved that their stated satisfaction with "the intelligence estimates they are now getting from his replacement" was misplaced. Item, from the *Times,* March 18, 1968:

> The Central Intelligence Agency has concluded that the enemy's strength in South Vietnam at the beginning of the 1st winter-spring offensive was significantly greater than United States officials thought at the time. . . . It puts at 515,000 to 600,000 men the force available to the enemy when the offensive . . . was launched on Jan. 30. . . . The so-called national intelligence estimate of the enemy . . . manpower in South Vietnam current at the time put the range at 448,000 to 483,000.

A difference of more than 100,000 men! Yet a story back on November 22 had announced: "WESTMORELAND SAYS RANKS OF VIETCONG THIN STEADILY."

December 27: "VIETNAM REPORT: THE FOE IS HURT." This story was written by the *Times*'s military specialist, Hanson W. Baldwin, a Washington-based journalist who was writing from Saigon, where he had gotten all the facts from those who manufacture them. The story began:

> The military indicators in Vietnam present the most dramatic and clear-cut evidence of progress in the war since the dark days of 1965. Victory on the battlefield has eluded the enemy. There seems little reason to doubt that Hanoi has abandoned the hope of conquest of South Vietnam by military force.

The contrast between the images projected by the statements of officials and by straight news stories coming out of Vietnam could be quite striking, as in the case of the following two items, which appeared only three days apart:

January 25 (Reuters): "PACIFICATION GAINS REPORTED BY KOMERS: The civilian leader of American pacification efforts reported today that 67 per cent of the South Vietnamese people now lived in areas secure from the Vietcong."

January 28 (Charles Mohr): "GENERAL'S MOVE PERTURBS SAIGON: Pacification Chief, Quitting, Saw No Hope of Success: The resignation of South Vietnam's pacification program has brought gloom to South Vietnamese and Americans here eager to see real progress in the Vietnam conflict."

And generally, as 1967 ended and 1968 began, the headlines began to tell a story increasingly at odds with the official picture:

December 8: "HEAVY SHELLING AT CONTHIEN AGAIN BATTERS MARINES."

January 9: "BISHOPS OF SOUTH VIETNAM, ASKING PEACE, SCORE THIEU."

January 11: "VIETCONG PRESS DRIVE FROM HIGHLANDS TO DELTA."

January 15: "SAIGON GROUP PROPOSES VOTE WITH LIBERATION FRONT."

January 26: "FORCE AT KHESANH IS FOE'S LARGEST."

January 29: "ENEMY FIREPOWER SAID TO INCREASE: Foe Reported Better Armed Than South Vietnamese."

And finally, almost poetically:

January 31: "VIETCONG INVADE U.S. EMBASSY IN SAIGON: Guerrillas Also Strike Presidential Palace and Many Bases."

On the same day that Hanson Baldwin's "The Foe Is Hurt" story appeared in the *Times* the Associated Press issued a story by its veteran Saigon correspondent, Peter Arnett. Arnett, winner of a Pulitzer Prize in 1966, has covered Vietnam as long as, if not longer than, any Western reporter on the scene. It has been claimed that he has seen more combat and certainly been on more operations than any Marine or GI and that he knows more about the country than any one American official in Vietnam. He sometimes indicates more knowledge and insight than American officials in their aggregate, as he did in the story entitled by the *New York Post,* "THE WAR: A REPORTER SUMS THINGS UP." The "summing up" is for the year 1967, and he predicts from it (compare officials' statements for the least inkling of this) that "the Communists have placed Westmoreland and his allies in what could well be a critical position in 1968." The story Arnett told was in most respects diametrically opposite that being fed the American people by official sources (and, lamentably, by many journalists and journalistic organizations who bought the line). Westmoreland's policy of "the war of attrition" was judged effective by the General, presumably on the basis of the kill-ratio he was receiving in Saigon and transmitting to Washington. But Arnett found that in the northern area near the DMZ, where official reports usually touted a large number of "enemy killed" in any given battle, the Communists had, through the year 1967,

> put to a severe test the allied tactics of attrition espoused by General William C. Westmoreland. At the DMZ, U.S. Marine officers estimated that casualties taken by both sides were on a *one-to-one basis all year long* [my italics].

Furthermore, as opposed to Westmoreland's statement about the steady thinning out of Vietcong ranks, the A.P. reporter wrote:

> Increased enemy capability may frustrate Westmoreland's plans to establish a fourth American corps headquarters at Cantho, in the Mekong Delta, early in 1968. Each of the delta's 16 provinces, except the Hoa Hao religious sect's province of An Giang, has as many armed guerrillas and Communist cadres as did the whole of Malaya at the height of its insurgency in 1950.

What is so astonishing in this whole story and its glaring conflicts of fact and fiction, of propaganda and reality, of persistence in ignorance and error, is not simply that it happened, but that it had happened so many times before, seemingly without any lessons having been learned. True, Westmoreland was "kicked upstairs" and replaced after the 1968 disaster. True, the Tet offensive of that year (and make no mistake about it) sealed Lyndon Johnson's political fate and forced the opening of the Paris talks, a veritable suit for peace for which the United States gave the required down payment: the limiting and then the halting of the bombing of North

Vietnam. But in the summer and fall of 1968 the new U.S. command, under General Creighton Abrams, was ringing the same old bell: The enemy had "shot his wad" and "run out of steam"; "significant progress" was being made, and the setbacks of February and March (seldom admitted previously) had been erased.

It is at this writing too early to tell if things will change significantly under the Nixon Administration, but there seems little reason to be overly optimistic about it, even if the war should be brought to a close. This is so because the malaise is not the personal characteristic of a single President or Administration; it is a structural, bureaucratic sickness that no Administration, short of virtual internal revolution, could significantly alter. It is true that Lyndon Johnson's own personality gave added impetus to the whole complex process of deceit and self-deception that is the Snow Machine. But he hardly invented it, and to this writer's knowledge no one dismantled it when he left office.

As should by now be clear, the Machine does not operate simply as a propaganda source; it also infects intelligence. We do not yet have, as do totalitarian countries, two separate, air-tight channels of information, one going from the field to the decision-makers, the second going from the decision-makers to the public. The Machine is structured on a tendency at every level to sell, or propagandize, not only the public but the level above it as well. The battalion commander stretches or invents his body-count; the division manipulates the figures that make up its kill-ratio; the embassy polishes up the political situation; the U.S. Agency for International Development edits its Presidential telegrams for excessive pessimism. And when the concatenation of all this fudging and hedging is not sufficient, instructions are received from Washington to lay it on thicker in the interests of political problems at home. The battalion commander in the field is not really trying to distort the picture; he is just trying to make his efforts look a little better. And if he doesn't, he is likely to be goosed by regiment or division, which have their own interests to advance, both those of the organizational ego and the careers of their commanding officers; and so it goes, up the line and across the board.

When Secretary McNamara traveled to Vietnam for his "fact-finding" visits, he was as carefully and deliberately processed through the Machine as George Romney or the average Congressman. His tours were carefully calculated and his briefings carefully rehearsed, not in order to give him a full and unadorned picture but to give him the picture that placed the efforts and personalities of those presenting it in the best possible light.* The commander in Saigon probably believes at least the basic outlines of the picture drawn by reports from his sub-units, but then he adds his own layer of deceit. If the reports from underlings do not provide sufficiently convincing "evidence" of the picture he wants to paint, he may either edit them or demand better reports, or both. And the same process takes place in Washington.

One lie, on this level of magnitude, compounds and reproduces itself geometrically. Lie A is sooner or later exposed. When that happens, lie B must be launched not only to shore up lie A but to explain the context in which the first lie occurred as an "apparent contradiction." Soon lie C is necessary to account for the discrepancies between lie B and apparent reality; and on and on it goes in a dizzy spiral toward madness—the same kind of spiral that could lead General Westmoreland to claim that the 1968 Tet offensive, even while its real dimensions were just becoming clear, was the enemy's "last gasp." It *had* to be the enemy's last gasp, because former lies had established that "the war of attrition is effective" and that "the foe is hurt." This spiraling insanity is both nourished and kept from becoming too blatantly obvious by the phenomenon known as the self-fulfilling prophecy. Thus, when the fiction of Diem's regime as a democracy supported by the South Vietnamese people began to be exposed by the lack of that support and outright rebellion, the specter of North Vietnamese control and

* In his book, *Our Own Worst Enemy*, William J. Lederer reported the following example (p. 35): "In June, 1967, U.S. officials in JUSPAO . . . held a meeting in Saigon. It was a tense and serious affair. They were making plans for Secretary McNamara's inspection tour of Vietnam. For three hours these public officials—whose job it was to help Secretary McNamara know the truth—discussed what they should let McNamara see, and who and what he should not see during his tour. An eyewitness told me that members of the United States Embassy, the U.S. military, and AID wanted to let McNamara learn only about things which would persuade him to approve their requests and policies, and withhold from him those things which might result in disadvantage."

infiltration was raised as explanation. When successor regimes were about to go down in defeat at the hands of South Vietnamese guerrillas and large-scale American intervention had to be ordered to save them, it was claimed that North Vietnamese units had tipped the balance and had to be matched. In truth it worked just the other way around: North Vietnamese units began to enter the South in significant numbers only after the Americans entered; the Vietcong had heretofore done quite nicely all by themselves.

The process also produces its own form of paranoia toward the public and particularly toward the press—the principle of "tattle-tale." A curious and frequent response from military and Administration officials (as well as from their more consistant private defenders) is to blame failures on the reporting of them. There is in this a kind of perverse lucidity, for it is often the public revelation of the lie which requires the bigger and more complex fiction and which tends to drive the process on to the next level. Be that as it may, the *definitive* exposure of the bigger lies in Vietnam is usually provided by events—which is to say, usually by the enemy, who pays scant attention to the output of the Snow Machine.

There is no question that the information received by Washington as a result of the Machine's workings is often erroneous, and sometimes disastrously so. Yet under Lyndon Johnson the Snow Machine was operated from the top with a cynicism equal to any employed on lower levels. According to Eric Goldman, a former Special Consultant to the President and most recently author of the book *The Tragedy of Lyndon Johnson,* it was the President, in reporting to the nation on the Dominican crisis, who transformed Tapley Bennett's already hysterical cable from Santo Domingo from "American lives are in danger" into "American blood will run in the streets" and who apparently fabricated the ludicrous tale of the American ambassador hiding under his desk while bullets whizzed through the windows as he talked to "his President." On Vietnam, Goldman offered this view of Johnson's attitude toward public information (as well as that of the State Department):

A large and complex literature has grown up about whether what was going on in Vietnam was in fact aggression in the customary sense of the word. The Johnson Administration scarcely added to the clarity of the debate; soon the State Department would issue a white paper, *Aggression from the North,* which was a ringing exercise in oversimplifications and questionable inferences. LBJ's attitude toward such documents was a smile and the assumption that these things were part of the complicated business of running a complicated country.

The significance of this vast intellectual corruption in Vietnam was eloquently articulated by Colonel Corson:

At a time when every thinking man is needed we are able to observe the spectacle of thousands of man days and nights wasted for no good reason. The corruption of purpose which occurs in the "hearts and minds" of our own people is serious. The U.S. press corps, which has tried to report accurately what goes on in Vietnam, has grown cynical as a result of the straight-faced official self-delusion and deception which is set forth as fact to any and all "interested" parties. Most of the nonsense and lack of understanding about Vietnam is a result of our official lying to one another. The compromise with the truth to achieve a greater good—perhaps to deceive the enemy—has produced a disaster.

■ CHAPTER 6 ■

Beat the Press

"Fuck your press cards!"
"Get the man with the camera!"
"Get the camera, get the photographer!"
"Give me that god damn notebook, you dirty bastard!"
"Beat the press!"
"Just wait, we'll get you."
"Give us your film or I'll break your head."
"I don't give a fuck who you are with."
"You take my picture tonight and I'm going to get you."
"Be careful—the word is out to get newsmen."
> *—Words spoken to or about newsmen by*
> *members of the Chicago Police Department*
> *during the week of the Democratic National*
> *Convention in August, 1968*

"Man, the pigs have gone wild. They're not after us;
they're after you!"
> *—A fleeing demonstrator to newsmen;*
> *same time, same place*

"The hostility toward any kind of criticism, and the fear of telling
how it is, has become too much, and it becomes our duty to speak
out. . . . The significant part of all this is the undeniable
manner in which Chicago police are going out of their way to
injure newsmen and prevent them from filming or gathering
information on what is going on."
> *—Chet Huntley on NBC radio; same time,*
> *same place*

—All of the above quoted from Rights in Conflict,
*the published report of the Chicago Study Team of the
National Commission on the Causes and Prevention
of Violence*

To some newsmen in Chicago that week there were strangely out
of place familiarities: remembered sights, sounds, and faces from
another world. These were newsmen who had worked the Vietnam
beat, and there were many of them in Chicago for the 1968 Democratic National Convention, where Vietnam most dramatically intervened in the internal affairs of the United States. Many of them,
old colleagues if not always old friends, hadn't seen one another
since this or that operation or the farewell party in Saigon. Such a
collection of old Vietnam hands was enough in itself to make the
superstitious feel a sense of foreboding. Contrary to the impressions
of many critics, the spearheads of the major media were seldom
men unschooled in the intricacies of political machinations or the
politics of strife and the distortions of battle. The television networks, in particular, which have come in for the greatest share of
criticism as a result of their convention coverage, fielded an impressive crew of correspondents who were not only veterans of
battles from the Ia Drang Valley to Khe Sanh but were also veteran
observers of Saigon politics and Buddhist street demonstrations
and riots and who carried, either on their bodies or in their memories, too many bipartisan bruises to be especially naïve about the
political process, whether it be by confrontation or by parlia-
mentary shell game.

They met at press conferences and caucases and in hotel lobbies
and lounges, and they shared the unsettling experience, a nagging
emotion, of seeing the dull-green "Huey" helicopters—visibly identical to the transports, ambulances, and "gun-ships" in which they
had so often ridden to and from war zones—circling the nation's
second city. They watched the barbed wire being layed around the
International Amphitheatre, just as they had seen it erected around
official American islands in Saigon. And they noted that it was
more difficult for a properly accredited newsman to get in and out

of the convention area than it was to enter and leave the American
Embassy or the Joint General Staff headquarters in Saigon. And by
the time the Illinois National Guard arrived in town, in spite of the
fact that the troops carried M-1's instead of M-16's, *"déjà vu"* had
become a cliché. Before the convention even got started, reporters,
cameramen, and photographers who had worked the Vietnam story
were painfully forced to recall the rifle-butts and clubs of South
Vietnamese troops which had broken their heads, ribs, and
cameras, and to remember the shouted imprecations that were very
likely Vietnamese versions of "Fuck your press cards," "Get the
man with the camera," "I don't give a fuck who you are with," and
"Beat the press." One even fantasizes that back on a muggy April
night in 1966, a young member of the Buddhist Struggle Forces
who was streaking past in flight from a skirmish line of combat
police or Vietnamese Rangers and was shouting something unintel-
ligible at newsmen as he went by might have been trying to say,
"Man, the pigs have gone wild. They're not after us; they're after
you!"

Although the business of shaping the news and controlling the
image of events which newsmen transmit has developed into a
highly sophisticated art in some quarters and at some levels, nothing quite so dramatically (and brutally) demonstrates the quin-
tessence of its purpose than a nightstick smashing a camera lens or
a policeman's hand clutching exposed film after a photographer has
been beaten to the ground. In the history of the Information War,
of the First Amendment, of the peoples' right to know, that must
remain one of the most salient contributions of Chicago during the
long, chaotic week of the 1968 Democratic National Convention.

Grosset & Dunlap, publishers of the report of the Chicago Study
Team of the National Commission on the Causes and Prevention of
Violence (dubbed the Walker Report after the team's director,
Daniel Walker), prefaced their book—*Rights in Conflict: Chi-
cago's 7 Brutal Days*—with an editorial comment that began:

> A foreboding of violence hung over the 1968 National
> Democratic Convention almost from the moment of its an-

nouncement. For months a conglomeration of dissidents had been promising in the national press that they would "turn the city upside down." They included all varieties of Marxist-Leninists, Maoists, violent and nonviolent revolutionaries, hippies, yippies, pacifists, New and Old Leftists, activists, followers of Senator Eugene McCarthy, idealists and cynics, and assorted camp followers of antagonism against the "establishment"—particularly against the convention machinery set to nominate Hubert Humphrey. . . . The city itself sweated nervously. In April of 1968 after Dr. Martin Luther King's assassination, Chicago erupted in violence. Mayor Daley enjoined his police to get tougher and, if necessary, "shoot to kill" arsonists and looters. [Actually, Mayor Daley's orders read "shoot to kill arsonists and shoot to maim looters"—though after the events of the "7 Days" that would seem an awfully nice distinction to ask the Chicago police to make.]

But the threat that hung over the Democratic convention had roots deeper and more varied than the preannounced activities of the Yippies and the National Mobilization Committee to End the War in Vietnam. A number of factors very nearly dictated the events of that week, both in the streets and in the city's International Amphitheatre itself—and most of them originated in or revolved about Vietnam: the growing public disenchantment with the war; the primary triumphs of Senator Eugene McCarthy and later of Robert F. Kennedy, who led an antiwar challenge to the Democratic Establishment which showed increasing momentum; the 1968 Tet offensive, which intensified both the public dissatisfaction with the war and the progress of the challengers of incumbent policy and which, in concert with the latter, forced Lyndon Johnson's retirement from the political scene; the increase in numbers and emotional dedication of young people, both those who worked actively for the challengers and those far more radically alienated from the conventional political processes; the assassination of Robert Kennedy in Los Angeles and the inevitable and increasingly obvious fact that the voice of the primaries would scarcely be heard in a convention organized and controlled by an orthodox party machine commanded by a highly defensive political establishment. Add to these factors the fact that Chicago is the most notoriously anachronistic epitome of the Machine Town, run by an all-power-ful mayor much as Lyndon Johnson had tried to run the national Administration. Add, finally, the recently adopted resolves of both national parties to limit press coverage of their conventions and to exert more control over the image the public received of these events.

The national conventions of the two major parties have long been the principal public spectacles (if not spectaculars) of American political life. Before the electronic era, however, they were spectacles only to the delegates and to the spectators from the cities in which the conventions were held. With the advent of live radio and television coverage (and especially with the latter) the business of selecting the party candidates was opened to the scrutiny of the public at large, thereby exposing the banality and superficiality of the events on the floor and making increasingly obvious to the general public the fact that the real decision-making took place in another part of the arena. TV reporters, made aware that the dull irrelevancies from the podium were turning off listeners faster than a blank television screen, began to hunt out more vital and interest-ing programming among the delegations and within and without the caucus rooms. At first the party structures welcomed such coverage as free publicity, but they soon began to learn that it bit as well as nourished, criticized as well as advertised, and, worse, had a tendency to show the two sides of the convention process—the public side and the sacrosanct, back-room side—as two seamy sides of a very soiled garment. Furthermore, television cameras and crews tended to get in the way of delegates and their managers, cluttering up the aisles and distracting the attention of the faithful from the official show on stage. Ultimately, it seems, party leaders decided live coverage hurt more than it helped, and though they couldn't quite ban it, they began to make an effort to limit and control it.

After the raucous 1964 convention that railroaded Barry Gold-water into candidacy before the eyes of millions of TV viewers, the Republicans vowed to restrict press coverage of subsequent conven-tions. The Democrats quickly followed suit, and both national conventions in 1968 drastically cut the number of press credentials issued. The cut was all across the board: Parking stickers, work passes, press platform passes, and floor passes were all reduced from the number issued at previous conventions. The Republicans cut the number of floor passes from 150 for the 1964 San Francisco convention to 100 in Miami. The Democrats, who had issued 200 floor passes in Atlantic City, permitted only 80 in Chicago. The three major television networks were permitted only one mobile floor camera each. The restrictions on the press in Chicago were not limited to the floor—they applied as well to work areas, observation galleries, and the general vicinity of the amphitheatre itself. And they applied downtown, far away from the convention's site, where press passes for the convention headquarters in the Conrad Hilton Hotel were equally limited. Making the situation even worse for the six thousand reporters, photographers, and radio-TV technicians who flocked to Chicago were the security precautions that made life all but unbearable for press *and* delegates even before the advent of physical harassment and general mayhem.

A strike by the International Brotherhood of Electrical Workers against Illinois Bell Telephone Company, which threatened to force the whole convention elsewhere, was conveniently settled at the eleventh hour by Mayor Richard J. Daley with a "moratorium" that allowed union members to wire only the International Amphitheatre; this effectively barred the installation of microwave relay facilities essential to live remote coverage from downtown, where the demonstrators would be. Furthermore, the networks' video-tape vans were not permitted to park in front of the hotels or to take up curbside positions elsewhere in the downtown area, thereby making more difficult even taped coverage of street events. For security reasons, cameras were not permitted on roofs, in windows, or on sidewalks outside the convention hotels. To Richard S. Salant, president of CBS News, it all formed "a pattern well beyond simple labor disputes, logistics, and security problems." And indeed, whatever the original validity of the labor disputes, logistics, and security problems, they were clearly used in an effort to limit press coverage and to control the proceedings of the convention itself. Limited telephone facilities permitted a great communications imbalance between the Humphrey machine and the opposition delegates committed to McCarthy and Senator George McGovern. Security agents on the floor of the convention were used to the same end, harassing opposition delegates and obstructing their efforts to communicate. Demonstration materials—placards, posters, and the like—were barred from the floor, except that Humphrey's forces had them in profuse quantity when it came time for his demonstration.

Security measures limited entrance to the amphitheatre to delegates, party officials and a few of their guests, small numbers of workers for the various factions, convention employees, and the press. Access to the building was gained only by means of small plastic cards, electronically treated, which were pushed into a slot in a metal box on which were two lights: one red, one green. Behind the box stood guards, watching to see which light your card activated. If it was the green one, your credentials were in order and you were OK. If the red one lit, you had a problem; either your card was a forgery (not treated), or you had entered before, left, and forgotten to "punch out." For reason of some mystical electronic process like charge reversal, one couldn't enter the building twice with the same card without having left it once properly. Also, there were different cards for different days and different cards for different purposes. A card with the proper hole near the top got you into work areas around the arena and permitted you to exchange it, for forty-five minutes, for another card that would get you onto the floor. Another (without the hole) gave access only to the work areas. Still another admitted you to the press gallery. The elaborate complexity of the process was downright awe-inspiring. (The chairman of the New Hampshire delegation, however, found a hole in the system. He discovered that a credit card worked in the little boxes every bit as well as the official credentials. On demonstrating this fact to a fascinated reporter, he was assaulted by security guards, manhandled, and dragged off under arrest, presumably for compromising security.)

Such was the atmosphere of the "Democratic" National Convention of 1968. Taking place in an enclosure surrounded by barbed wire and amidst a host of guards, policemen, and security agents who seemed to outnumber the delegates, the event struck some observers as more reminiscent of an election of the Soviet Presidium than of anything they had witnessed on the American political scene. With all this, one can imagine the surprise of press and delegates alike when a throng of local denizens, dragooned by Mayor Daley from the city's streets and bars, filled the press gallery, entering the amphitheater with nothing more than the torn halves of paper hotel passes hanging around their necks (reporters bearing proper credentials for the gallery were barred from it on several occasions). Daley's minions were used to counter demonstrations by opposition delegates on the floor and to hoot it up for the mayor ("We love Daley!" "We want Daley!"), who was beginning to take a lot of verbal lumps—not only from the press but from speakers on the platform.

As for the general picture of the proceedings, it is difficult to decide whether that is best symbolized by the arrest of the New Hampshire chairman and his credit card or by the image of Richard Daley drawing his forefinger across his throat in a signal to the platform to cut the floor mikes or to adjourn the session. In terms of the press story the signal event of the convention itself will probably remain the stomach punch delivered to CBS's Dan Rather on camera, live coast-to-coast and in color, by a security man right there in the middle of an event that is supposed to symbolize American democracy, which is offered as a model to the less-civilized world.

The result of Lyndon Johnson's soured consensus was a convention in which delegates were treated like cattle and newsmen like rustlers. The young demonstrators who came to Chicago, however, were treated like an invading army. Whatever the felt need or purpose of the restrictions, harassment, and intimidation of opposition delegates in the amphitheatre, the fact remains that most, easily a clear majority, of the delegates to the 1968 Democratic National Convention came to nominate Hubert H. Humphrey as the party's Presidential candidate. In the face of the results of several major primaries since the first of the year, that majority had already been prefabricated by party machines in states where no direct primary was held. McCarthy and Kennedy may have won the primaries and indicated the mood of registered Democrats, but most analysts agreed days before the convention opened that the challengers hadn't a chance and that HHH had it in the bag.

It was this loud and clear situation that motivated many young people to come to Chicago, in spite of warnings of violence, to protest, among other things, what they felt to be an intolerable discrepancy between the will of the rank-and-file and the response of the party leaders, the Establishment. That violence was not only possible but probable was evident very early, not so much from the stated intentions of the more radical and activist demonstration leaders as from the paranoid reactions of city officials, led by their mayor. The most comically absurd put-ons were accepted as challenges to the continued existence of civilization. An alleged threat (almost undoubtedly made) to put LSD in the city's drinking water was apparently received with the utmost seriousness by men who were seemingly unaware that at current market prices the cost of purchasing an amount of LSD sufficient to hallucinate the population of Chicago would run into the tens of millions of dollars. That there were people among the demonstrators intent upon provoking violence is undeniable. That they could have saved themselves the time, energy, and expense of the trip, since the Chicago police were ready, willing, and able to do their work for them, is a matter of record. The denial of parade permits, the seriousness with which the most nonsensical threats were received, the obvious rage with which Richard J. Daley reacted to the prospect of demonstrations in *his* streets against *his* convention, as well as the mayor's recorded impatience with police restraint, made a violent confrontation almost inevitable. As Dick Daley inadvertently commented in a news conference following the convention: "Gentlemen, get this thing straight for once and for all. The policeman isn't there to create disorder. The policeman is there to preserve disorder [*sic*]." There is a statement that should earn Richard J. Daley a secure place in American social and political history ("Fuck you!," which he clearly shouted at Senator Abraham Ribicoff during the convention proceedings, was not original with the mayor and consequently doesn't qualify) and deserves the unrelenting jealousy of writers all across the land.

However the role of the police is described, the part played by

Chicago cops during convention week, 1968, was painfully apparent to reporters and photographers who covered the proceedings in Lincoln Park, Grant Park, on Michigan Avenue, and in other downtown *loci* of the street action. The Walker Report states that forty-nine newsmen were hit, maced, or arrested, "apparently without reason, by the police." The report goes on to say that "in ten of these incidents, photographic or recording equipment was deliberately broken" and that "in over forty instances, the newsman involved was clearly identifiable as such. . . . In only four situations do the facts indicate that the newsmen were so mixed in with the crowd that the police could have hit them under the mistaken apprehension that they were demonstrators." The report's section on police-press violence concludes with the statement that other attacks on newsmen occurred but were not included in the study because of insufficient evidence.

Newsmen have been kicked, shoved, beaten, maced, even shot by police officers many times before, but probably never in such numbers as in Chicago during the last week of August, 1968. And never before has such action received such carefully detailed investigation as that given the Chicago affair by the Walker Report. The findings of the Study Team's investigation are painfully and explicitly illuminating:

> Approximately twelve policemen were standing around watching. Sequeira [Paul Sequeira, a Chicago *Daily News* photographer] began photographing the incident [an AWOL soldier, in uniform, beating a white uniformed doctor who was an intern at a Chicago hospital]. At least two policemen approached him saying, "Get out of here." Sequeira showed his press card and shouted "Press." He was hit on the helmet, arm and back by police and forced to his knees. Suddenly his helmet was on the ground. Sequeira tried to use a camera to fend off the blows to his head. . . . His right hand was broken and he had head injuries.

> DeVan [Frederick DeVan III, a *Life* magazine photographer] . . . said he heard someone shout, ". . . get the camera, get the photographer," and a policeman wearing neither badge

nor name tag appeared on his right and broke his camera and two viewfinders with the butt of a shotgun.

He [Claude Lewis, a reporter for the Philadelphia *Evening Bulletin*] . . . was wearing convention credentials and a press card about his neck. He had seen police beating a girl and stopped to take notes. According to Lewis, an unidentified patrolman stepped forward from a police line along the curb saying, "Give me that god damn notebook, you dirty bastard." Then the policeman grabbed the notebook, tossed it into the gutter, and clubbed Lewis four or five times on the head, knocking him to the ground.

Together they grabbed him, swore at him and searched his pockets, taking a roll of exposed film. They then started to grab his cameras, threatening to smash them. One policeman was heard to say, "Give us your film or I'll break your head."

As he [Robert Jackson, a Chicago *American* reporter] started to get up, he showed his press credentials. Jackson says the policeman replied, "That don't mean a damn thing to me, nigger," and clubbed him on the right shoulder, leg and on his buttocks and back. He quotes the policeman as saying, "Get your black ass out of the alley."

Actually, the motivation of the policemen described and quoted above differed from that of Richard Daley and John Criswell (LBJ's convention hatchet-man and master, with Daley, of the convention machinery) only in their slightly more primitive directness. David Brinkley summed it up on NBC when he opined: "The Democratic leadership does not want reported what is happening."

It was all, of course (to borrow Sartre's evaluation of the 1956 Russian intervention in Hungary), worse than a crime; it was stupid. The effort of Mayor Daley and his officials to safeguard the image of "Daley City" was to scar and blacken that city's image more profoundly than could have been imagined. And given the very narrow margin with which Richard Nixon won the 1968 Presidential election, it is neither original nor daring to suggest that the high-handed repression and intimidation at the International Amphitheatre and the "sanctioned mayhem" (*Time* magazine) in the streets cost Hubert Humphrey the election. To city and party officials, however, it was not their own actions but "press bias" and "biased coverage" which caused the etching of the image. With the continued deliberate attacks by police on newsmen and indiscriminate attacks on anyone in sight, news executives and organizations across the country reacted with outrage, both officially and editorially, and commentators and columnists did likewise. *The New York Times*'s Russell Baker wrote that "the only people who can possibly feel at ease at this convention are those who have been to a hanging." And Hugh Downs, on NBC's *Today* show, asked what else Chicago's police could be called but "pigs." Reacting to Downs's crack, Frank Sullivan, Chicago police press-officer, held a news conference during which he described the demonstrators as "a pitiful handful. They have almost no support. But, by golly, they get the cooperation of the news media." As had happened so often in Vietnam, the men in charge were blaming their blunders and failures on the reporting of them—a full circle.

After fulminating against press "distortions," Daley had his own distortion produced by one Henry Ushijima. Entitled "What Trees Do They Plant?," this hour-long official version of events in the streets was given national television exposure in September by the Metromedia network. It was, in fact, considerably better done than most of Daley's critics expected. The film's producer chose not to emulate his patron's strident frenzy and to use instead a low-key rhetoric and a format that included one or two mildly dissenting views. Its action scenes, however, were almost invariably taken from far behind the "front line" and carefully avoided any visual indication (as it avoided mention) that cops had gone after reporters, footage of which the networks had in profusion. In addition, credence of the discriminating was marred early in the film when scenes of the demonstrators peacefully lounging in the park were hyped with a riot soundtrack recorded during subsequent clashes with the police—a rather clumsy effort at subliminal communication. Not a single scene in the film showing provocation of the police by the demonstrators had not already been shown by the networks during the week of the convention. In the end "What Trees Do They Plant?," in its inability to make any significant rebuttal to earlier press coverage, only dug Chicago's pit a little deeper. The Walker Report, clearly unaffected by "Trees," summed up the events it described in two words: "police riot."

■ CHAPTER 7 ■

Reaction and the New Manichaeans

"Nothing is ever any different from how it ever was except these punks get publicity."
—John Wayne, quoted in *Time* magazine, August 16, 1968

This plaintive statement, a combination of belief, wishful thinking, and scapegoatism, represents the feelings of a far greater number of Americans than eastern intellectuals like to think, particularly of middle- and lower-class Americans whose values and verities are discarded and discredited almost wholesale by their own children in a time of racial unrest, civic decay, and global uncertainty. The press is a natural scapegoat partly because it sometimes seems to defend and give aid to the enemy (or a host of enemies), partly because of the obviousness of many of its own shortcomings, but mostly because of a psychological quirk common to citizen and politician alike which holds that a thing isn't really and fully so until somebody says it—an atavistic reversal of the primitive belief that to learn the name of a thing was to control it. The press, the liberals, and the Left may have been unanimous in their condemnation of Richard J. Daley and the Chicago police, but the greater portion of the American public did not join in that unanimity. The weight of their support fell instead with the mayor of Chicago and his police. Daley's mail was reliably reported to be running 20 to 1 in his support, and a similar clear decision was registered in the mail sent to newspapers, radio and television stations, and networks during and following the week of the convention. It was also reflected in what was surely one of the two most important issues (and probably *the* most important issue) of the 1968 campaign, "law and order," an issue all three candidates in the Presidential election emphasized in their own separate ways.

Whatever damage the press had done the Johnson Administration's credibility in reporting Vietnam or Santo Domingo or other stories foreign and domestic, it had not survived without scars of its own. At whatever low ebb of popularity, the President retains a great influence with most Americans, as does the apparatus of his national Administration, and the defensive and retaliatory operations of the Snow Machine have at times cut deeply into the credence that many Americans give even their favorite newspapers and radio-television stations and networks. At times of particularly sharp contradiction between government assertions and press reports all much of the public knows for sure is that somebody is lying; and for very many, if not most, it is much more difficult to believe such a thing of the President and responsible officials than of a reporter or commentator. When, in the emotional atmosphere of a bitter war, the Secretary of State publicly asks reporters, "Which side are you on?," millions of Americans have confirmed for them a suspicion that the press is in some way subversive to the country itself.

In December of 1968 NBC broadcast a documentary entitled "The People Are the City." A generally excellent program on racial and poverty problems, it was marred in one significant respect: A major section of the documentary, dealing with a black section of Boston, was only sketched in—done, as it were, with a telephoto lens. In explantation Frank McGee, the narrator, told a story that had become very familiar to urban reporters and news organizations in the past two years. Organized community groups refused to let NBC's crews film that section of the program—refused cooperation and promised demonstrations if the network went ahead without that cooperation—unless leaders of the groups were granted power in the selection of participants for that portion of the program and in its editing. NBC, not surprisingly, refused.

With the increasing radicalization of the civil-rights movement, at least from 1966 onward, white reporters found it increasingly uncomfortable and often downright impossible to cover the activities of the more activist and militant civil-rights and Black Power organizations. They were frequently denied entrance to meetings and rallies and sometimes ejected from those they had been able to enter. Black reporters, on the other hand, working for the same organizations, were not interfered with as a rule. This was partly due to a deliberate and highly successful strategy to force room for Negroes in a profession that had remained suprisingly white while known for its support of civil rights and integration. But the development had another aspect: a generalized and growing mistrust and outright antagonism toward the "white press" and its coverage of the black community. And by 1968 NBC could no more do their Boston segment with black reporters and crews than they could with white ones.

There is, one must admit, some justice in this attitude. But right or wrong, it is indicative of the extremely difficult situation in which the press finds itself as the political polarization of American society proceeds. The hostility white reporters found among southern whites earlier in the decade is matched by the hostility of urban blacks today, though it has for the most part a different source and a different character. The usual hostility of Right Wing groups toward reporters is now matched by the hostility of much of the Left. The major news-gathering organizations—the main body of American journalism—are generally lumped together, no matter how disparate their editorial directions or their front-page policies, by the more radical groups. To the white racist it is the "integrationist" or "liberal" press. To the black militant it is the "white" press. To the Right it is the "leftist" press; and to the Left, the "Establishment" press. For all, however, it is the enemy's press.

A new Manichaeanism emerges. The Manichaeans, who thrived from the third to the fifth centuries before being denounced as heretics and extirpated by the Church, were one of several early religious sects that preached a doctrine of radical dualism: God and the Devil are coeternal and constantly at war, and all matter and men belonged to one or the other. There are two, and only two, categories: good or evil, light or darkness, and so on. The innate dualism at the heart of Christianity caused offspring of these sects to spring up in spite of Church repression. The crusade against the dualistic Albigensian heresy opened the era of the Inquisition. The doctrine of radical dualism returned in the twentieth century in a secular guise; and ironically, it was the philosophical descendants of the Albigensians and Manichaeans who presided over the inquisitions of our time. One of the central experiences of the last fifty years has been that political, social, and racial doctrines of radical dualism are lethal to democracy, whether managed by a Hitler, a Stalin, a Joe McCarthy, or by the latter-day Manichaeans of our own period. In a truly polarized or radicalized environment the neutral or "objective" observer finds himself alone and surrounded by enemies, for both sides define "enemy" as "those who are not one of us." The neutral or middle ground is the first to go, for dualism demands an abyss between the poles—an abyss that grows larger and larger, contemporary history teaches us, as each camp begins to feed progressively on the fringes of its own membership.

What makes the present situation somewhat alarming is that the hostility toward the press common in radical politics has become more and more apparent at the political center, or among those who formerly occupied the political center—which is to say, among the formerly apolitical or politically apathetic masses of Americans. The white middle and working classes, frightened by high crime rates and ghetto unrest, threatened by black demands for a decent share of the pie, confused and outraged by their strange, wild children, are fueling polarization, and hostility toward the press, at a rapid rate. An instructive example of this polarization and some of its effects on the press was offered in New York City by the 1968 teachers' strikes and by the anti-Semitism controversy surrounding radio station WBAI-FM, with which the author was for several years associated as a correspondent and, subsequently, as program director.

The New York teachers' strikes of 1968 grew out of an attempt to decentralize the city's massive educational bureaucracy and to apply the principle of "community control" to its public schools. The main target of this experiment was the abysmal educational showing of ghetto schools, one of the earliest and most important arcs in the closed circle of noneducation-deprivation-despair which afflicts the ghetto dweller, chiefly black and Puerto Rican, and his children and his children's children. Community members would vote for their own local school boards, which would have limited independence from the city-wide board of education in tending to the educational needs of the community's children. The Ocean Hill–Brownsville section of Brooklyn, an almost entirely black area, was chosen as a demonstration district along with other sections of the city prior to the approval of a general decentralization plan by the New York State legislature. The experiment almost immediately clashed head-on with the teachers' union, the United Federation of Teachers.

One of the principal complaints of black ghetto parents about ghetto schools is what they feel are the essentially racist attitudes of many white teachers and administrators toward their children, and the new governing board of Ocean Hill–Brownsville was not slow in taking the offensive in this area. In May, 1968, the board transferred nineteen white, mostly Jewish, teachers from the district who they felt, justly or unjustly, were not fit to teach black children. Albert Shanker, president of the U.F.T., called the action "Nazism." When the schools reopened in September after summer recess, the U.F.T. struck the entire city school system.

The principal issues in the confrontation were, on the part of the governing board, the right of the community to hire and fire (or transfer) the teachers and administrators in its schools and, on the part of the union, established due process and job security. Underneath these issues, however, was a class conflict endemic to the ghetto and crucial to the racial and poverty problems of our urban areas. Like the white merchant and the white landlord, the white teacher has long been seen by the black and Puerto Rican ghetto resident as an agent of internal white colonialism and exploitation who is working, consciously or not, to extract from him as much as possible for as little as possible and to keep him in his place and condition—which is impoverished, uneducated, and helpless. On the other side, white teachers view Negro demands for more black teachers and administrators and more control over schools in black areas as threats to their own livelihood and economic security. Very much the same process created the "white backlash" among blue-collar workers in response to demands for meaningful integration of the building trades and other laboring occupations. On an organizational level, the United Federation of Teachers saw the fragmentation of authority and responsibility posed by decentralization as a distinct threat to the power of the union. An added factor, which was to become almost the last straw, is the fact that a majority of the white teachers in New York City are Jewish, which provided the significance of the "Nazism" charge.

Actually, 1.8 million New Yorkers are Jewish, comprising the largest Jewish community outside of Israel. The Jewish community, if such it can be called, and especially those of its members in the teaching profession, had long been in the forefront of liberal and progressive movements and causes in the area and made up the largest single ethnic grouping in the Northeast so involved. In the early, "southern" stages of the civil-rights movement Jewish young people comprised not only the largest single ethnic or religious element among white civil-rights workers but an easy majority of white civil-rights workers. The murder in Mississippi in 1964 of two Jewish young men, Andrew Goodman and Michael Schwerner, along with James Chaney, a Negro, was accurately symbolic of that representation. It was not (or should not have been) surprising, then, that in 1965 and 1966, when the more militant civil-rights groups began to insist on Black Power—black leadership and control of the movement—and even the expulsion of whites from leadership positions, charges of "reverse racism" and "anti-Semitism" were heard, charges given added weight by the influence on some black radicals of Frantz Fanon (the anticolonialist theoretician and author of *The Wretched of the Earth*), the Algerian revolution against the French, and the plight of the Arab masses and their hatred of Israel.

The three teachers' strikes in the fall and winter of 1968 were caused and complicated by a number of factors: a city plan that established the demonstration districts but did not spell out the powers granted to them; a union position that was essentially inflexible (as was that of the governing boards) and which, underneath all the propaganda, was against all meaningful decentralization long before the immediate issue of the strikes, the transfer of the nineteen, had occurred; and finally, but far from least, the explosive racial element in the situation. The latter was present in the very nature of the ghetto and in the reason for its existence; it was present in an economic and educational situation that produced many white teachers and administrators but few black ones. The deeply rooted, institutionalized racism that permeates our society and keeps the greatest part of an entire race within the confines of the lowest class was the most significant target of decentralization in ghetto areas. This, combined with the feeling of many teachers and of those who supported them that changes in the educational system as it affected the ghetto dweller were being made at their expense, caused a reaction identical with that of backlash.

The clash between the union and the parents inevitably became a clash between white and black (though many white teachers supported the governing boards and continued to teach during the strike). And because a high proportion of the white teachers were also Jewish, it became a conflict between blacks and Jews (even though many of the white "scabs" were Jewish). The union responded to black demands from the outset by crying "Nazism" and "anti-Semitism" in an effort to galvanize the powerful Jewish community in the city and enlist its support of the teachers. That support was for a long time conspicuous in its absence, but the trick worked, and New York City was soon in the grip of racial hysteria, an hysteria shared by political leaders, to whom the Jewish vote is crucial. The major Jewish organizations fell over one another in their haste to denounce both "black anti-Semitism" and decentralization itself, and new organizations sprang up to do the same. When David Spencer, chairman of the I.S. 201 Complex governing board (a Harlem demonstration district), complained about this reaction, he himself was accused of anti-Semitism. The charge against Spencer, by the Anti-Defamation League, was the result of a letter he had written in October, 1968, in which Spencer stated the obvious as an explanation of the growing anti-Jewish feeling among blacks. In the words of the Anti-Defamation League, quoted in an article by Walter Karp and H. R. Shapiro (the article,

published in the newsletter *Public Life* in February, 1969, excori-
ated Shanker, the U.F.T., and the whole anti-Semitism hysteria),
"Spencer said . . . it is hard to keep from reacting against everyone Jewish when the full weight of the Jewish Establishment is not
only beating our black and Puerto Rican communities, but also
accusing us of being the aggressor." Karp and Shapiro commented:
"Here is a man openly and manfully complaining about organized
Jewish efforts to use anti-Semitism as a weapon *against* him, and for
that he is charged with anti-Semitism. If you want to create anti-
Semites, *that* is as good a way as any to start." The escalation of the
decentralization issue onto the plane of "racism" and "anti-Semitism" had been accomplished, and the resulting polarization drew
forth expressions of white racism and black anti-Semitism (actually
more of the former) on a scale heretofore unknown in the city's
recent history.

During the same period the New York Metropolitan Museum of
Art opened a show called "Harlem on My Mind," a photographic
history of Harlem. The catalog of the exhibit was prefaced with an
essay by Candice Van Ellison, a Negro high-school girl. Miss Van
Ellison, who had by that time graduated, had written the essay as
part of a school project, and it had later come to the attention of
the catalog's editor, a Jew. Mayor John V. Lindsay joined Jewish
organizations in denouncing the essay as anti-Semitic. The sections
in question dealt with black attitudes toward Jews and other groups
(Irish and Italian) that had formerly been ghetto dwellers but that
now, to the black man, were part of the white majority. Even on the
face of it, it appeared that the mayor and the Jewish organizations
demanding the catalog's withdrawal were labeling as "black anti-
Semitism" what was essentially an attempt to describe and explain
the sources of black anti-Semitism. The story became almost ludicrous when the news broke that the passages most seriously being
attacked had originally been quotations, properly footnoted, from
the book *Beyond the Melting Pot,* by Daniel P. Moynihan and
Nathan Glazer, who is a Jew himself, and that it was at the request
of another Jew, the editor of the catalog, that the girl had dropped
the quotation marks and reworded the passages to read as her own
work. Those revelations, however, were lost in the din of hysteria.

They may have embarrassed some of those involved in the attack on the museum, but none of them ever admitted it in public, nor did the accusations subside because of them. Ultimately the museum's director, Thomas P. Hoving, was forced to withdraw the catalog. Interestingly, and relevant to the theme of polarization and of the plight of the "middle man," black writers, artists, and political activists found the exhibit at the Metropolitan a superficial, white man's view of the ghetto, and many of them picketed the show.

On Thursday evening, December 26, 1968, WBAI-FM broadcast the reading of an undeniably anti-Semitic poem written by a fifteen-year-old school girl at J.H.S. 271, in the Ocean Hill–Brownsville demonstration district. WBAI is a noncommercial radio station supported by subscriptions and contributions from its listeners (or a small percentage of them) and is one of three such stations owned and operated by the Pacifica Foundation. Although it has no editorial position per se, its programming drift tends to be liberal and even leftist, with an emphasis on public affairs and news. Its audience, particularly its paying subscribers, tend to reflect that drift and is largely made up of middle-class liberals, college students, and professionals, including teachers—many of them members of the United Federation of Teachers. Furthermore, that audience is composed of a high proportion of Jews, as in any liberal grouping in New York City. The station, in its function as a news organization and in its educational capacity, has long been involved in the cause of civil rights and has heavily programmed the manifold issues and incidents pertaining to that struggle. In line with this and in keeping with the policy of the Pacifica broadcasting group, the station made active efforts to open its microphones to people who ordinarily are not given a public hearing. One of the cornerstones of the founding philosophy of Pacifica was the concept of a "free marketplace of ideas" of the air, and consonant with that the stations have always offered a broad range of political and social commentary and opinion covering the entire spectrum, from the Right to the Left, from the American Nazi party to the Communist party—or have tried to do so. In order to provide a broadcasting platform for the expression of those who are less known, less articulated, have no access to the media, and whose thoughts and opinions are consequently not heard by the public at large, the stations have incorporated the live telephone format into some of their regular programs. One such program was the Julius Lester show, "The Great Proletarian Cultural Revolution." Lester, an extremely talented black writer, journalist, and musician, conducted the program—part music and part talk, both in the studio and on the telephone—for two hours each Thursday night, from 9:30 to 11:30.

On the Thursday night in question Lester had Leslie R. Campbell as a guest on his show. Campbell, a black teacher from J.H.S. 271, was a prime target of the U.F.T. and its president for allegedly "harassing" U.F.T. teachers. The discussion centered on the teaching of black children, the development of pride in themselves and in their race, and the development of self-expression. The discussion also inevitably dealt with the issues of the strike and its effect on the children. Campbell had brought to the studio several poems written by students, and three of these he read on the air. The second of the three, expressly entitled "Anti-Semitism" and dedicated to Albert Shanker, read in part:

> Hey, jew boy with that yamaka on your head,
> You pale faced jew boy, I wish you were dead. . . .
> When the U.N. made Israel a free and independent state
> Little four- and five-year-old boys threw hand grenades.
> They hated the black Arabs with all their might
> And you, jew boy, said it was alright.
> Then you came to America, land of the free,
> And took over the school system to perpetrate white supremacy. . . .
> I hated you jew boy, cause your hang up was the Torah
> And my only hang up was my color.

Clearly, the poem is both an expression of anti-Semitism and an attempt to explain it. There was an expected reaction to the reading when the program moved into its latter period and telephone calls were taken on the air, but it was surprisingly light and low-keyed. A number of letters protesting the reading came into the station in the course of the next week, but these, too, by and large, were fairly reasonable and written by regular listeners and subscribers who were familiar with the station. The following week Lester devoted the entire two hours of his program to continuing the dialogue that the reading of the poem had begun. Conducted largely on the telephone, the dialogue included both blacks and Jews and ranged over the issues of "black anti-Semitism," the teachers' strike, and the effects on black children and Negroes in general of the blatantly antiblack racism expressed on the U.F.T. picket lines and in union statements that used such terms as "mob rule" to describe decentralization. Letters on the subject, commenting on the controversy from a number of points of view, continued to come into the station, but in diminishing numbers. By the end of the first week in January the issue seemed to be dead. A total of thirty letters had been received on the issue—hardly a flood—and nearly a third of these, many from Jewish listeners, supported Lester and the station, if not Leslie Campbell.

On January 16, 1969, the following story appeared on the front page of *The New York Times,* headlined "TEACHERS PROTEST POEM TO F.C.C.":

> The United Federation of Teachers has complained to the Federal Communications Commission about an anti-Semitic poem read over a local radio station by Leslie R. Campbell, a controversial Negro teacher in the Ocean Hill-Brownsville school district. . . .
> A spokesman for the teachers' union said yesterday that it had written to the Federal Communications Commission "expressing our vigorous protest that WBAI-FM was being used to spread anti-Semitic propaganda in general and attacks against New York teachers in particular. . . ."

It was at this point, three weeks after the program in question, that a veritable storm broke on WBAI (which had been one of the few media outlets, along with *The Village Voice,* that had consistently pointed out the union's exploitation of "anti-Semitism" in its propaganda and warned about the likely effects of such political arson). An avalanche of letters poured in protesting the broadcast as reported in the *Times*. Every major Jewish organization in the city, with one or two exceptions, followed the lead of the U.F.T. The New York Council of Rabbis, the national Anti-Defamation League, the American Jewish Congress, the American Jewish Committee, the Workmen's Circle, and the Jewish Defense League demanded the Federal Communications Commission take steps against WBAI ranging from public hearings on the issue to outright extirpation of the station—the revocation of its license. These organizations were joined by powerful non-Jewish groups and personages in the demand for WBAI's scalp. The City Club of New York echoed the cry; Francis X. Smith, chairman of the City Council, demanded an F.C.C. investigation with a view toward license revocation; Emanuel Celler, U.S. Representative from Brooklyn, chairman of the House Judiciary Committee, and a politician who knows the value of the Jewish vote better than he knows the wording of the First Amendment or the Federal Communications Act, wrote the F.C.C.: "I consider the action of the directors [of WBAI] an abuse of the broadcast license granted to them and I urge that the Federal Communications Commission use its full powers under the law to redress this abuse of the public trust."

A curious, and I think highly significant, semantic development took place at this time. It occurred in many of the letters the station received, in the texts of organizational protests to the F.C.C., and even, in one case, in the comments of a journalist. Bob Williams, television critic for the *New York Post,* stated that WBAI had abused its First Amendment *privileges.* Free speech and free press had, overnight, been downgraded from rights to privileges! As for the Celler letter, a broadcast license is, of course, a privilege, not a right. But the Federal Communications Act expressly extends the protection of the First Amendment to the holders of that privilege. Congressman Celler resolved that apparent contradiction by downgrading, as had Bob Williams, the First Amendment itself. He charged that the directors of WBAI had "attempted to shield themselves with a *mistaken interpretation* of the First Amendment [my italics]." The obvious implication here was that the scope of the First Amendment stopped short of protecting such public utterances as the poem. And many of the groups and individuals involved in denouncing WBAI agreed—or felt that if it did not stop short of such protection, it should. Some critics applied the well-known dictum of Justice Oliver Wendell Holmes that freedom of speech does not extend to shouting "Fire!" in a crowded theater. WBAI answered that the dictum could only be applicable in the absence of fire, which was manifestly not the case in New York City in the fall and winter of 1968–1969.

The station, of course, deplored anti-Semitism as it deplored antiblack racism and had long been actively involved in exploring and fighting them. In the two years preceding the controversy it had broadcast over 260 separate programs dealing seriously and constructively with these issues. But all that was of no avail. The situation had been polarized beyond rationality. WBAI was anti-Semitic, in spite of the past (and current) record of the station, in spite of the fact that more than two-thirds of its staff were Jewish, in spite of the fact that the president of Pacifica was a Jew and that four out of seven members of the station's board of directors were Jewish! But the most profoundly frightening aspect of the whole affair was the rapidity and near unanimity with which, in a highly emotional, polarized atmosphere, some of the most liberal groups and individuals in the nation were willing to scuttle the First Amendment. In a long article in *The Village Voice,* "The Siege of WBAI," the author and journalist Nat Hentoff spelled it out:

"There is no doubt, certainly, that life in the United States remains freer than in the Soviet Union," Edgar Friedenberg writes in the February *Atlantic Monthly.* "What is doubtful is that our greater freedoms express the will or would even be acceptable to it." For example, what is the general will in this city with respect to WBAI? I would fear to make that station's fate the subject of a popular referendum. . . . In these recent weeks, those who have been importuning the FCC to punish— better yet, to obliterate—WBAI have been remarkable and chilling in their quantity and respectability.

But perhaps not so remarkable if Friedenberg is right, and I think he is. Introduce the Bill of Rights to the New York City Council—without imprimatur of its place in the Constitu-

tion, typing it instead on Commonweal stationery—and . . .
the overwhelming will of that body would be swift and clear.

Fortunately, the F.C.C. refused to succumb to this hysteria. It
dismissed the U.F.T. complaint and, by association, the others,
finding that such statements as those expressed in the poem, repel-
lent as they might be, *are* protected by the First Amendment. The
commission's statement to the press also cited the station's past
record and present intentions in the field of race relations as
reasons for dismissing the complaints.

Interestingly, during this same period a complaint against WBAI
was filed with the F.C.C. by a pro-Arab organization that charged
the station with being pro-Zionist. When the Jewish Defense
League presented the station manager with a number of demands,
one of which was that Lester be fired, they were told they would
have their answer in twenty-four hours, after the board of directors
had had a chance to examine them. The board rejected the demands as being out of hand. But one group of New Leftists,
engaged at the time in attacking the station because it had been
"taken to the Right," saw perfidy in the delay. The manager had
copped out, said they, in not making the decision himself on the
spot.

More important than these relatively unimportant incidents, the
liberal-Left community in the New York area, which WBAI once
served as a fairly homogeneous audience, was increasingly dividing
itself into those who thought the station had been captured by the
far-out fringes of Black Power and the New Left, and those who
were convinced it had drifted, or been pulled, rightward into the
gravitational field of the Establishment. A statement by a commentator that WBAI was not the handmaiden of the Left brought
howls from those who held that it should be. The presence in the
program schedule of a regular commentary by spokesmen for the
Black Panthers convinced others that the station had become the
propaganda organ for that end of the spectrum. Neither group was
willing to concede WBAI its own position, its separate function,
independent of their views and dogmas.

WBAI survived the worst of the crisis, albeit considerably

bruised and shaken, and the anti-Semitism hysteria receded, at least temporarily, as summer and the end of the school year approached. But the incident indicated, as had Chicago, the extreme vulnerability of the First Amendment in the highly emotional atmosphere of political and racial polarization. It has been said that people usually get the kind of government they deserve. A corollary to this observation would certainly be that in a democracy people will retain only those rights and freedoms they are willing to grant others—however distasteful and even painful that might be. Furthermore, as previously suggested, a growing intemperance toward such freedoms and toward the activities of the press, protected in the First Amendment as a cornerstone of the democratic system, may well indicate a growing impatience with the tensions and strains of democracy itself. And few politicians, it should be evident, are likely to resist for long the erosion of confidence in the First Amendment safeguards among their constituencies.

If this trend needed further documentation, it received it, along with increased impetus and dimension, on November 13 and again on November 20, 1969, when Vice President Agnew attacked first the networks and then the printed press, ironically co-opting what had heretofore been largely a liberal critique of the media to mobilize the "silent [largely conservative] majority" and to discredit, if not intimidate, liberal critics of President Nixon's policies. Agnew's assault on the press and its implications for the future of that institution will be dealt with in the following chapter. Here it is sufficient to observe that it was probably one of the most politically successful harangues, at least in the short run, of any in recent American history. Writing in the November 28 edition of his paper, *Times* columnist James Reston reported what the networks had already had to admit, that

> letters coming into *The New York Times* are overwhelmingly favorable to Mr. Nixon and Mr. Agnew and sharply, even savagely, critical of the press and networks. Most of these letter-writers are saying that they are with the President and Vice President, and they are charging the press and networks with embarrassing the Administration and helping the enemy. But quite a few of them go beyond this into a general indictment of

reporters and commentators—often lumped together as if their assignments were the same—for "stirring up trouble" among the poor, the blacks, and the rebellious young on the university campuses.

The incident at Songmy became a major and sustaining news story literally on the heels of Agnew's attack on the networks. Little more than a week later, Mike Wallace interviewed a twenty-two-year-old disabled Army veteran named Paul Meadlo for CBS News. Meadlo admitted to having taken part in the massacre and recounted the incident in some detail. It was, to be sure, a searing, harrowing performance, in which the seemingly less than bright veteran answered the question of how he, the father of two children, could kill babies in their mothers' arms with the line, "I don't know, it's just one of them things," explained his participation in the slaughter by saying, "It just seemed like it was the natural thing to do at the time," and complained about the cut in his disability allowance by the Veterans Administration (subsequently he complained that he had not been paid for his CBS interview and vowed not to talk any more unless he was paid). Curiously, public response to the interview in the form of phone calls and letters did not overwhelmingly denounce the massacre or what seemed the moral obtuseness of the young veteran but rather Mike Wallace and CBS for airing the interview! A *New York Times* reporter* found that Meadlo's home town, New Goshen, Indiana, regarded him as blameless, most of those interviewed excusing him by observing that "after all, he had his orders." "The only thing I blame Paul David for was talking about this to everybody on television," said one local citizen. If this town in the heart of middle America is a fair representation of the "silent majority," a poll of the attitudes of Americans toward the Songmy affair and its public exposure might prove a very frightening document, much more so than Agnew's speech. It is the awakening of this sleeping dog of provincial ignorance and bigotry which has rightly concerned many commentators and columnists more than any implied threats of government action against the press contained in recent attacks by the Nixon Administration.

* J. Anthony Lukas, *The New York Times,* November 26, 1969.

■ CHAPTER 8 ■

Government and the Partly Free Press

"The problem is that the Establishment doesn't want to share that information [repression in Chicago] with the public. They've always profited by being able to control that information and knowing where the sources of the information are and what was happening in advance of the public. Now they don't know in advance any longer. They learn it and the public learns it simultaneously. And this is where the problem is. This is why the Establishment is trying to put the clamps on us."

> —Walter Cronkite, speaking on the Public Broadcast Laboratory documentary "The Whole World Is Watching"

Although many Democrats may have been dismayed at what happened in and around their convention in Chicago, the reaction of a great many Congressmen and Senators, both Democratic and Republican, was to echo to one degree or another the reaction of Richard Daley and to come down hard on the press for distorting events. Official outrage was largely focused on network television coverage, though most newspapers and wire services told essentially the same story and showed much the same pictures. There were two basic reasons for singling out television for congressional wrath:

(1) It has far greater impact, emotionally, than the print media, and greater distribution than all the daily print media combined.

One national poll indicated that two-thirds of adult Americans cite television as their major source of news.

(2) The print media are substantially protected, at least at present, from governmental incursions, retaliation, and control by the First Amendment. Radio and television are not. Their news operations obviously come under the heading of "press," but their very existence is technically at the government's pleasure and can be revoked. The Federal Communications Act of 1934 reserves ownership of the airwaves to the public and charges the Federal Communications Commission to grant licenses "in the public convenience and necessity." In addition, radio and television licenses are not granted permanently but must be periodically renewed. Passed in the adolescent days of radio, the Communications Act was a necessary attempt to regulate the absolute chaos of a new and unrestrainedly proliferating medium, access to which is limited by the finite number of broadcast frequencies. Furthermore, the act specifically states: "Nothing in this act shall be understood or construed to give the commission the power of censorship over the radio communication . . . and no regulation or condition shall be promulgated or fixed by the commission which shall interfere with the right of free speech by means of radio communication."

In point of fact, the commission has been generally careful to honor that proscription, and what censorship does occur in the electronic media (and it is massive) is both self-imposed and, in the past, has had little to do with government pressures or control. Nevertheless, the machinery for governmental control of program content is there, the authority of government in broadcasting is long established, and its retaliatory power is considerable. There is an inherent contradiction in the guarantee of First Amendment rights to a medium licensed and regulated by the government; but although it is difficult to see how it could be otherwise, licensing has always been a prime instrument for controlling the press, and when in force, it is always available for that purpose whether it is used or not. Indeed, the slow development of the free press in English culture could be dated from 1695, when the licensing laws were repealed, or perhaps from 1644, when John Milton published his *Areopagitica,* an eloquent attack on those laws and their use to restrict free speech and press. A broadcast license is granted by the government to a radio or television station as a public trust and a privilege. As long as that is the case, radio and television news departments will never enjoy the full rights and protections guaranteed by the First Amendment; they will always constitute a partly free press.

The Communications Act itself documents the contradiction. It rules out the power of censorship and then proceeds to establish it. As an example, obscenity and profanity are proscribed in broadcasting, and the F.C.C. is charged to enforce that proscription, violation of which may cause a station to lose its license. Now, of course, there are laws prohibiting obscenity in the printed media as well, but they are nowhere nearly so stringently interpreted and applied as is that section of the Communications Act, and they are (with the exception of the sending of obscene material through the mails) local statutes, not federal laws. Freedom of speech is, and always has been, construed as less than absolute, and the First Amendment has traditionally been interpreted by the courts as drawing the line of its protective covering short of certain forms of speech and writing. The point is that the protected area drawn by that line is far smaller for broadcasting than for the other media. Much that is now easily conceded as permissible for books, magazines, newspapers, even motion pictures, remains a restricted area to broadcasting. That such a limitation can be relevant to broadcast news was made evident during and after the Chicago convention bloodletting, when apologists for the police described the liberal use of obscene epithets by the demonstrators as a major provocation. For most newspapers the deletion of quotes of those epithets was simply a question of taste (though a questionable journalistic practice). For most broadcasting organizations it was also concern for the penalties provided by the Federal Communications Act.

If the F.C.C. generally seems to honor the limitations placed upon its authority by the Communications Act and the First Amendment, its record is not an altogether consistent one. Consider, for example, an F.C.C. ruling of September 25, 1968, which prohibited the broadcasting of lottery advertising and information. Though the language was somewhat vague, the ruling apparently also prohibited editorials in favor of a state lottery, formerly a major public issue in the state of New York, which now has such a lottery. At this writing the ruling is being challenged in the U.S. Court of Appeals; but whatever the outcome of the case, it seems clear that the F.C.C. had attempted to outlaw broadcast editorials on a question of significant public importance.

In another case the F.C.C. announced on March 20,1969, that it was withholding license renewal of KRON-TV in San Francisco, a station owned by the San Francisco *Chronicle,* pending investigation into charges that the station had managed news programs to promote the corporate interests of its newspaper owner. It seems an awkward case for those interested in preserving the strengthening of the First Amendment in broadcasting. One applauds the intent of the commissioners, and yet their action against a particular kind of pattern in news content or format raises some interesting questions concerning censorship. Does a federal agency, prohibited by law from exercising "the power of censorship over the radio communication," have the right to censor a private censor? If the answer must be yes, it should not be given without an awareness of the dangers of its implications. Censorship and the power to regulate are like metal and magnet—they are hard to keep apart—and to keep the latter relatively distant from the former requires a high order of vigilance. Late in 1968 press censorship was formally abolished in South Vietnam in belated accordance with the country's recent constitution. Yet in the course of a few months thirty-two Saigon dailies were suspended, either temporarily or altogether, for publishing stories displeasing to the government, the government having retained that *regulatory* privilege. It is not altogether inconceivable that on some dark, repressive day in the future, "public convenience and necessity" could be interpreted in Washington in the same manner that "national security" is currently interpreted in Saigon.

The concern of the TV networks when, after Chicago, the public seemed to turn against them and influential Democratic officials and Congressmen filed complaints with the F.C.C. was understandable. On March 2, 1969, the commission cleared the networks of charges of "bias" in covering the story, hastening to add that its decision related only to the question of "fairness" (representing all sides in a controversy) and did not address itself to the question of whether network coverage presented "the truth" of events shown. The commission stated that although it considered the "truth" in news coverage important, such an essentially subjective judgment by a government agency would be "inconsistent with our concept of a free press," and it added: "The government would then be determining what is the 'truth' in each news situation—what actually occurred and whether the licensee deviated too substantially from that 'truth.' . . . We do not sit as a review body of the 'truth' concerning news events."

On the other hand, the commission announced that it was still investigating charges of incidents "staged" by television camera crews, indicating that all aspects of "truthfulness" were not outside its purview. Like managed news, the question of staged scenes presents some sticky legal and philosophical dilemmas and uncovers some rather basic inconsistencies in governmental regulation of broadcasting. For instance, government officials are constantly requesting news management in their own and in what they call the "national" interests. And it is yet to be reported that the F.C.C. is investigating Metromedia for the "staging" done in "What Trees Do They Plant?" by Daley's sound-man. Perhaps it is felt that the program qualified as entertainment rather than as news. Though the practices of management and staging are undeniably professional sins and unethical, the assumption by the government of the power and responsibility for judging the professional and ethical conduct of newsmen is difficult to reconcile with the F.C.C.'s statement about the propriety of judgment by a government agency on what is the "truth" about news events. This would seem equally "inconsistent with our concept of a free press."

The problem is a fairly recent one and rises out of the confluence of several contemporary trends, one of them, ironically, a more liberal and responsible attitude on the part of the F.C.C. toward its responsibilities. For much of its existence the Federal Communications Commission has been justly criticized for being little more than an industry lobby in the executive branch of government. Its members and its succession of chairmen have been far too closely associated with the industry to view it with the detachment required of a regulator, and its actions have seldom questioned, much less threatened, the *status quo* in broadcasting—until recently. In the decade of the sixties younger, generally more liberal commissioners, with fewer ties to the industry itself, have prodded the commission toward a more activist role in the regulation of American broadcasting. Increasingly the commission began to concern itself with the abysmal use to which television's immense potential had been put, the dominance of banality, the tyranny of commercials, the problems of fairness and of access to the media for people whose views run counter to the attitudes of its operators and their commercial sponsors, and with the effects of monopoly and media conglomeration on broadcasting. The commission may have evidenced a kind of bureaucratic schizophrenia on a number of occasions, reflecting its own sharp divisions on the issues, yet it has shown increasing concern for the flowering of the First Amendment in broadcasting.

Another trend, perhaps equally ironic, has been the opening of television—however slight, timid, tentative, and even temporary it may be—to more freedom for content and controversy, more sophisticated and relevant programming in both news and public affairs and in entertainment. It is a very small move, but nonetheless a move, away from the very lowest common denominator.

The Congress, like the F.C.C., has traditionally been almost slavishly responsive to the expressed interests of the broadcasting industry, and individual Representatives and Senators have always been cognizant of the importance of good relations with broadcasting outlets that serve their constituencies. The relationship has been reenforced by the fact that a number of Congressmen have extensive financial interests in broadcasting. One of them, Clarence Brown, Jr., not only owns a daily newspaper and an FM station in his district but is also a member of the House Commerce Committee, a subcommittee of which is the House communications "watchdog."* Even so, a subtle change has begun to take place in the attitude of Congress toward broadcasting. This change may in part be due to the fact that F.C.C. rulings on fairness, "equal time," and

* *Straus Editor's Report,* June 21, 1969.

"personal attacks" have made the individual politician less vulnerable to hostile broadcasting outlets and decreased the importance of their goodwill. But an equally significant reason may be the indications of a growing public mistrust of and disenchantment with the media, especially the broadcast media, so strongly registered in the aftermath of Chicago. Last but far from least in a Congress dominated by Democrats must come the political wounds of the Vietnam war and the salt rubbed in them by press coverage of the 1968 Chicago convention. In the weeks and months following that convention a number of hearings and investigations into the television coverage of Chicago were initiated, both on the federal and on the state level. The Congress empowered the National Commission on the Causes and Prevention of Violence to subpoena executives from the three major networks. The House Investigations Subcommittee investigated unused network TV footage from Chicago for possible use in hearings by the House Communications Subcommittee, and the state of Illinois conducted its own investigation.

Shortly after the F.C.C. cleared the networks of biased coverage of the convention (or at least declined to rule on the matter), the Senate Commerce Committee's Communications Subcommittee, led by its chairman, Rhode Island Democrat John O. Pastore, began hearings into violence on TV. It is a subject with which many Americans are, and should be, concerned. The Senators, however, did not confine themselves to violence in television entertainment shows. Senator Pastore, an elderly Italian Catholic, proceeded to demand the imposition of his own rather parochial concepts of decency and good taste on television programming, charging "salaciousness" and "irreverence" and demanding more self-censorship in a medium that is already literally choked in self-censorship. Jack Gould, writing in the March 17,1969, edition of *The New York Times,* reported:

> While violence on TV shows, and cigarette commercials, have tended to pre-empt recent Washington headlines on broadcasting, Senator Pastore and some of his colleagues have made clear that they are no less concerned with the over-all moral tone of the medium, particularly in matters of electronically pro-

jected sexiness and outspoken quips on the Pope and birth
control on such shows as "Laugh-In" and the "Smothers
Brothers Comedy Hour."

Clearly, the new freedoms in television programming, however
small, were not to Pastore's liking, nor did his remarks evidence
much reverence for the Constitutional doctrine of the separation of
Church and State. The Senator from Rhode Island was not making
a private request when he ordered network executives quite per-
emptorily: "Clean up the filth!" There was clearly an "or else"
implied, not only in his tone but in the power of his position and the
fact of the proceedings themselves.

The F.C.C., in the meantime, had been making an almost revolutionary effort to break up the logjam in commercial television and
radio. In a move designed to encourage greater diversity in the
medium, the commission resolved to take more than the standard
pro forma look at license-renewal applications and at challenges to
those renewals. On January 23, 1969, the commission denied the
renewal application of WHDH-TV in Boston, a station affiliated
with CBS and owned by the Boston Herald Traveler Corporation,
publisher of the daily newspaper of the same name. The purpose of
the new policy was to crack down on the huge multimedia con-
glomerates that have been progressively monopolizing the nation's
communications media over the years and, in the words of Commissioner Nicholas Johnson, to open the door "for local citizens to
challenge media giants in their local community at renewal time
with some hope of success." Senator Pastore, however, apparently
worried only about the institutionalization of his own prejudices,
offered the broadcasters a *quid pro quo:* In exchange for further
internal, "voluntary," censorship, he would oppose such F.C.C.
action. As Gould pointed out, "He linked a purge of program
material with comforting reassurances that he would fight for the
economic security of licensees." The industry demonstrated its
courage and dedication to principle by inviting the Senator to speak
before the 1969 convention of the National Association of Broadcasters. There, Pastore repeated a proposal, made at the time of the
hearings, that the N.A.B. set up machinery to review and pass on

network programs prior to broadcast. A majority of the broadcasters accepted with embarrassing alacrity. Holding up his part of the bargain, Pastore then went to work on a bill that will, if made law, prevent the F.C.C. from considering license challenges without having first established that the holder of the existing license is not operating in the public interest. In effect, such a law would all but rule out competition for previously issued licenses.

Commercial broadcasters, whatever their protestations to the contrary, are seldom truly concerned with freedom of program content (freedom of commercial content is a different matter) when the pressure is on and when the money is on the line.* And it requires the greatest amount of charity to assume no connection between Senator Pastore's remarks and the cancellation of the "Smothers Brothers Comedy Hour," an event that followed the Senate hearings by less than a month (the show was one of three singled out for specific denunciation at those hearings).

There was another, perhaps far more significant, aspect to the Pastore hearings: They concerned themselves not simply with violence in television entertainment but also with violence in TV news and in coverage of public affairs. One item of evidence placed in question was the TV footage, in full color and sharp sound, of the summary execution of a young, disarmed Vietcong officer in the streets of Saigon by the commander of South Vietnam's National Police, Brigadier General Nguyen Ngoc Loan. It was a shocking, brutal scene. But it is also one of those scenes for which television is preeminently valuable, for it cut through all the statistical and rhetorical cant and presented to the viewer, in the space of a moment, the unadorned horror of that war. It may also have had something to do with the ultimate political demise of General Loan, a security-police commander in the tradition of Heinrich Himmler

* Although the three major television networks stood firm (at least at the outset) against the Nixon-Agnew attack on their news operations, network affiliates and many independent stations across the country reacted otherwise. CBS President Frank Stanton, in an address given in New York following Agnew's second attack, deplored the fact that whereas the industry had reacted strongly on the national level, the Vice President's remarks had had considerable effect at the local level. He cited the case of one local station that announced it would, in response to Agnew's criticism, no longer carry analyses following major addresses but would return immediately to its regular programming.

and Russia's Lavrenti Beria. But more important, that and other scenes from the 1968 Tet offensive—the ugly image of American corpses piled like cord wood on the backs of tanks and personnel carriers, the bloody bitterness of Hue and the insanity of Khe Sanh—shocked Americans into a new awareness of the Vietnam war and forced them to reexamine America's participation in it. The sense of "being there," of "seeing it with your own eyes," provided by television, had a profound effect on the conscience and consciousness of Americans of many political persuasions. Some military people will argue that for this very reason television should be curtailed. But the First Amendment's provisions for the protection of a free press were meant precisely to provide the public with this kind of information about the actions of government.

The Loan incident was not the first, or even the most horrendous, story of its kind in television's coverage of the war. Other executions have been filmed and shown—this reporter was personally present at one filmed by cameras from all three major networks, when South Vietnamese Marines shot a Buddhist prisoner in Danang in 1966—as has the torture of prisoners by South Vietnamese troops in the presence of blasé Americans, the systematic destruction of villages, and the mutilation of enemy corpses. But none of these had quite the psychological impact of Loan's execution of the Vietcong officer, coming as it did in the midst of an enemy offensive that caught the American public thoroughly unprepared.

Curiously, on the Public Broadcast Laboratory documentary quoted earlier, Senator Pastore opined that government censorship "can never happen." The Senator stated that he didn't think "the Congress can legislate about what can be shown and what cannot be shown, no more than we can . . . question the editorial policy of a newspaper." To do so, he said, would be to run "smack into the First Amendment." What, then, was the justification for the Senator's subcommittee investigation into violence on television? On the same P.B.L. program Richard Doan, a critic for *TV Guide*, reported that "the Congress, according to the information I get, is madder than the dickens at television at this point [after Chicago]. The reporters who covered Congress for many years say that they never knew a time when there was so much hostility toward television. . . . They would like to do something, but they don't know quite what to do." Senator Pastore and his colleagues, however, knew very well what to do. They knew that there is much to be accomplished by indirection which cannot be done directly. The method might be called the handle technique, one familiar to prosecutors. Many criminals, known to be guilty of crimes from narcotics trafficking to murder but immune to successful prosecution due to a lack of proper evidence, are finally put away for lesser violations, such as income-tax irregularities. Policemen frequently lock up on vagrancy or loitering charges people who are suspects in cases with too little evidence to warrant arrest or to whom they have simply taken an aversion. A variation on the handle technique, applicable to Pastore's actions, is commonly known as bribery. The F.C.C. had, unknowingly, provided the Senator with just the leverage he needed.

A classic example of how the First Amendment in broadcasting can be attacked, from behind as it were, was a case involving, once again, WBAI and its parent organization, the Pacifica Foundation, which, because of their essentially unorthodox nature and frequently outspoken, contentious, and genuinely controversial (a candidate for one of the decade's ten most misused words) programming, have on a number of occasions served as a kind of lightning rod for the industry in the area of free speech. The Pacifica Foundation began in 1949 as a single FM radio station, KPFA, in Berkeley, California. Throughout the McCarthy era, with the exception of one brief hiatus, the station broadcast what was by any measure the most provocative and varied programming to be found on either dial or screen in that period of craven timidity. Generally left of center both in the persuasions of its staff and in the content of its programs (after all, free speech was, at least then, almost exclusively a Left Wing issue), the station, curiously enough, was never descended upon by the various state and national bodies operating to sterilize all aspects of political life and thought at the time, though it fully expected that would happen. The probable reason for this uncharacteristic lack of zeal on the part of the Inquisition was that a single FM station, operating in Berkeley, California, was just not that important. In 1959, however, Pacifica began to operate another station, serving the Los Angeles area, and in 1960 the foundation began to take on the dimensions of a small network when it acquired a formerly commercial channel in New York City, WBAI. Now the noncommercial outlet that had the temerity to put Communists on the air with fifteen-minute commentaries, to broadcast largely uncensored contemporary poetry and plays and also documentaries on such topics as homosexuality, had stations in three of the largest population centers in America. And one of them was in the opinion-molding capital of the nation. Varying complaints were lodged with the F.C.C. beginning in 1959, ultimately resulting in an unprecedented three-year postponement of license renewals for all three stations. But the big crunch did not come until 1963.

In October, 1962, New York's WBAI produced and broadcast a two-hour interview with a former agent of the Federal Bureau of Investigation, one Jack Levine, who blasted, with an insider's information, the activities of the bureau in general and the despotism of its director, J. Edgar Hoover, in particular. Realizing the explosive potential in such an exposé, the producers of the program carefully checked Mr. Levine's authenticity through both the bureau and the Department of Justice and sent transcripts to each, offering opportunity to comment or respond. Asked why he had brought his story to WBAI rather than to a larger, more influential press organization, Levine answered that he had literally taken it everywhere: to the wire services, to *The New York Times,* to other newspapers, and to other radio-television outlets—none of them would touch it. Friends of the station in the press and in the legal profession warned that the broadcast of the program would almost certainly mean a lot of trouble and might even cost WBAI its license; J. Edgar Hoover and the organization he ruled were thought to be sacrosanct and assailable only at great risk. After considering the advice and the consequences that advice warned of, the station decided it had no choice but to go ahead with the broadcast. The program was subsequently broadcast and rebroadcast on all three stations. The day following the New York broadcast both the *Times* and the wire services, which had turned the story down until WBAI broke it, ran it extensively, the *Times* in a front-page article. Subsequently, KPFA, in Berkeley, broadcast a second program (also heard in Los Angeles and New York), which consisted essentially of corroboration of Levine's charges by another ex-F.B.I. agent, who added a few kicks of his own.

Late in December the Senate Internal Security Subcommittee, headed by Connecticut Senator Thomas J. Dodd, announced that it had subpoenaed executives of the Pacifica Foundation and would hold hearings into suspected Communist affiliation among its principals. The hearings were held in Washington in January, 1963, with Senator Dodd piously disclaiming any intent to scrutinize programming and then proceeding to ask question after question concerning program content, participant selection and identification, including questions about the Levine program and the names of those responsible for producing it and those involved in the decision to put it on the air. In an obvious attempt to strike at the foundation's financial base, the subcommittee subpoenaed a Los Angeles *subscriber* who the investigators alleged had Communist connections. The tactic was one that had already been tested and patented at the height of the McCarthy era, when Americans became so frightened of putting their names on petitions or organization lists that one particular petition circulated on the streets of New York City got only rejection and hostile comments, some charging the circulators with being Communists or "pinkos"; the petition was a paraphrase of the Bill of Rights. To this day, all three Pacifica stations receive contributions, usually the price of a subscription, from people who send the money anonymously because they do not want to be on subscription lists.

In any event, the subcommittee discovered nothing and ultimately published the transcript of its hearings without comment or recommendation. Thus the S.I.S.S. had gone as far as it could, and now the pressure was on the F.C.C. to finish what the Senators had started. It was the opinion of a number of Washington observers who were close to the case that such pressure had been actively applied. Even if that were not true, the very fact of a Senate investigation into a radio station would normally constitute a certain amount of pressure for the commission to look into the case itself before license renewal, if only as a matter of form. But there is a more important aspect in the passage of such an investigation from one body to another. For a Senate subcommittee to instigate action in such a case (beyond passing the file along to a federal agency) it must make a fairly clear finding of some form of documented culpability. The F.C.C., on the other hand, when issuing or renewing broadcast licenses, must make a positive finding as to the fitness of the applicant and whether or not the licensee's broadcast performance, past or intended, is "in the public interest." It can, therefore, act on far less solid ground. Furthermore, it is the F.C.C. that controls all the "handles," i.e., regulations concerning obscenity, profanity, and a host of technical requirements and violations.

In the technical area, almost any radio or television station is, from occasionally to frequently, in minor violation of F.C.C. regulations, and in the program area almost anything can bring letters of complaint to the commission. This is particularly true of any attempt at probing or controversial programming. Such letters are added to the file of the station or licensee kept by the commission, which may or may not require a response from the licensee. On the basis of such response the F.C.C. may find in favor of the licensee and dismiss the complaint, or it may find in favor of the complainant. If the latter, it may then do one of several things: It may issue a simple reprimand, it may impose a fine, it may hold hearings, or it may suspend, revoke, or refuse renewal of the license. These are, of course, the necessary teeth of any effective regulatory agency. The point is that there are many "handles" in the F.C.C. and fairly wide discretionary powers the commission can use in determining what is or is not "in the public interest." The situation is made more serious by the fact that the F.C.C. like most federal agencies (excepting the F.B.I. and the military), has tended to be a political shuttlecock, generally moving in the direction of the greatest amount of pressure.

On January 22, 1964, after deferring the three stations' license renewal for three years, the commission finally exonerated Pacifica and renewed its licenses. The reasons for the findings on each of the three points in contention (obscenity, Communist infiltration, and the transfer of authority) were copiously explained in the commission's order granting renewal. But the real reason was that friends of the First Amendment and of Pacifica had been able to generate more pressure than Senator Dodd and his friends; the real issues involved in the investigations, both that of the Senate subcommittee and that of the F.C.C., were clear not only to those at Pacifica, but also to much of the nation's press. Newspapers and magazines across the country, led by the influential *New York Times,* came to the defense of the listener-sponsored network in their editorials and attacked both the Dodd subcommittee and the F.C.C. for what seemed a transparent assault on the exercise of the freedoms of speech and press in broadcasting. (The response of the broadcasting industry was a thunderous silence.) There seemed little doubt that in the view of some significant national powers Pacifica's general program policies and performance were "out of line." And with Levine's attack on Hoover and the F.B.I., it had just gone too far. The central issue was straight First Amendment and the freedom of the press enshrined in it—an amendment governmental bodies have not always resisted trying to shove aside when they could not afford to run "smack into" it.

The issue was never more explicitly stated than by the F.C.C.'s chairman at the time, William Henry. In April, 1964, after the commission had cleared Pacifica of all charges, Henry spoke at the annual convention of the National Association of Broadcasters (the one area of the press from which Pacifica did not receive editorial support—or support of any kind) and shocked his audience with an excoriating indictment of the broadcasting industry's silence during the affair, its lack of courage, and the double standard with which it viewed the First Amendment. He admitted the commission had been wrong in withholding Pacifica's licenses, but he told the broadcasters that he held them equally to blame. He compared the industry's storm of protest when the F.C.C. sought to limit the number and length of radio and television commercials to its evident lack of interest in Pacifica's plight—a genuine free-speech, free-press issue.

Which state association sent delegations to Congress charging that the F.C.C. had deferred the Pacifica licenses for an unwarranted period and was operating outside its jurisdiction? Which of you wrote me a letter urging the commission to dismiss these charges and to reaffirm the commission's time-honored adherence to the principles of free broadcasting? Where were your libertarian lawyers and their *amicus* briefs, your industry statesmen with their ringing speeches?

If broadcasters felt involved in this issue, there is no evidence in our records to indicate these feelings. Apparently not one commercial broadcaster felt obliged to make his views known to the F.C.C. When you display more interest in defending your freedom to suffocate the public with commercials than in upholding your freedom to provide provocative variety, when you cry "censorship" and call for faith in the founding fathers' wisdom only to protect your balance sheet, when you remain silent in the face of a threat which could shake the First Amendment's proud oak to its very roots, you tarnish the ideals enshrined in the Constitution and invite an attitude of suspicion. You join the forces of crass complacency—in an industry and at a time in the history of this nation when complacency of any sort is both misplaced and dangerous.

Henry knew where it was at, on both sides of the track. But although the F.C.C.'s ultimate decision in the Pacifica case was something of a broadcasting milestone ("We recognize that as shown by the complaints here, such provocative programming as here involved may offend some listeners. But this does not mean that those offended have the right, through the commission's licensing power, to rule such programming off the airwaves."), the facts of the case were clearly that the F.C.C. had been used to attack Pacifica for *reasons* that unmistakably flouted the First Amendment on *grounds* that technically did not, at least as initially interpreted. This potential availability of the regulatory machinery for manipulation and abuse cannot help but add to the timidity of the broadcasting industry and to its concern when the Congress is unhappy with coverage of a political convention, sex and violence on entertainment shows and commercials, or satirical remarks about the Pope.

The November Offensive

Liberals generally applauded what seemed, at least for a time, to be a new resolve on the part of the F.C.C. to irrigate the vast wasteland and to stimulate greater diversity and independence in the broadcast media. For the same reason they generally opposed Pastore's efforts to protect the holders of broadcast licenses from competitive challenge. What most tended to overlook was the potential use of precedent set by an "activist" commission if that agency came under the rule of a philosophy less respectful of the First Amendment. The Nixon Administration's 1969 November Offensive against the press, however, provided the liberals with a sharp reminder. Quite pointedly, following Nixon's November 3 address to the nation on his Vietnam policy, the new F.C.C. chairman, Dean Burch (a Goldwater campaign aide in 1964), personally called the three networks and asked for transcripts of commentators' remarks on the speech. Next came Agnew's November 13 blast in Des Moines, Iowa, reminding the networks that they were licensed and regulated by the government. Subsequently, in an action that was interpreted (misinterpreted, in this writer's view) as something of a retreat, Burch said in effect that the networks, in providing commentary and analysis following the Nixon talk, had not violated the commission's fairness doctrine. A point generally missed, however, was that for the first time in the history of that doctrine it had, if only informally, been applied to comment on the President and his policies. And although Administration officials made a halfhearted effort to deny that censorship was their goal or intimidation their intent, antagonists of the press with more freedom to say what they meant began to crawl out of the woodwork in considerable numbers.

Probably the most outspoken of these was Senator Thomas J. Dodd, Democrat from Connecticut. Dodd suggested it was time for a "first-class inquiry" into the power of the press. Following Agnew's second attack, in Montgomery, Alabama, on November 20, Dodd charged that *The New York Times* had used its power to overthrow governments friendly to the United States and had brought unfriendly governments to power—though he offered no examples.* (Presumably he had in mind the *Times*'s successful overthrow of Cuba's Fulgencio Batista and the installation of Fidel Castro, clearly a *Times* puppet.)

But one of the most striking and ironic spin-offs from the November Offensive, and one that revealed the depths of the quandary into which the liberals had been thrown, was the assertion by Senator John O. Pastore, made in an interview by Christopher Lydon, of the *Times,* that the Agnew attack had helped the chances of his (Pastore's) bill. Lydon observed that whereas the Senator earlier had "advocated the bill principally on the ground that the growing number of license challenges threatened the economic stability of the broadcast industry," he presently considers "what he views as a threat of political pressure on television news and of politically motivated license awards by the Federal Communications Commission . . . an even more compelling reason." Pastore indicated that he now expects new support from the liberals. The Senator from Rhode Island, who had previously ordered the networks to "clean up the filth" and to censor satirical treatment of the Pope, now observed: "Apparently the liberals have now become sensitive to the implications. The former Vice President [Humphrey] has called the Agnew speech an attempt to stifle expression and thought. Now those are the things that were on my mind in this bill."† As though to resolve any questions of consistency, the Senator continued, "How are we going to preserve the independence of this industry so that, *within the bounds of morality and decency* [my italics], they can think as they like and say what they think?" How, indeed!

Agnew's Des Moines address was a classic weave of outright misstatements of fact, distortion, half-truths, and, it must be emphasized, full truths, the whole pattern designed to discredit critics of the Nixon Administration and its policies. To fully appreciate its thrust and importance as an Administration move, however, it must

---

* *The New York Times,* November 22, 1969.

† John O. Pastore, quoted by Christopher Lydon, *The New York Times,* November 20, 1969.

be seen in the larger context of a series of government moves, dating from the last year of the Johnson Administration, to discredit (and when possible to punish) the leaders and organizers of active dissent against the Vietnam war and to discourage or intimidate real and potential followers.

In January, 1965, a federal grand jury handed down indictments against the so-called Boston Five (the Rev. William Sloane Coffin, Jr., Michael Ferber, Mitchell Goodman, Marcus Raskin, and Dr. Benjamin Spock) for "a continuing conspiracy to aid, abet, and counsel violations of the Selective Service law." The charge surprised many laymen who had always considered "conspiracy" a plotting of covert things in dark places. But the government's case rested on a series of overt and quite public acts, and the wording of the indictment was so broad as to include, potentially, anyone who applauded one of the defendants at a peace rally or assisted in the spreading of their opinions: "The defendants herein did unlawfully, willfully, and knowingly combine, conspire, confederate, and agree together and with each other, and with diverse other persons, some known and others unknown to the Grand Jury."

A pamphlet entitled "A Call to Resist Illegitimate Authority," written in 1967 by Arthur Waskow and Marcus Raskin as a statement of declaration, was printed in the *New York Review of Books* and circulated around the country as a petition, picking up around 28,000 signatures. This petition is discussed in the Foreword to *Dr. Spock on Vietnam,* a paperback published by Dell Books, and it became Overt Act No. 1 in the indictment. In her excellent book *The Trial of Dr. Spock,* Jessica Mitford wrote that she had shown the Justice Department's John Van de Camp a copy of the book and asked him if Dell could be charged as part of the conspiracy.

" 'I imagine Dell, *technically,* could be liable; conceivably they could be prosecuted.'

" 'And the booksellers?'

" 'Yes, and the booksellers.' "*

Continuing her line of questioning, Miss Mitford asked John

---

* Jessica Mitford, *The Trial of Dr. Spock* (New York: Alfred A. Knopf, Inc., 1969), p. 70.

Wall, the government prosecutor, about the scope of the conspiracy net:

> He answered that the law is clear: that anybody who gives *encouragement* . . . can be so considered. So, I asked, the man who claps and cheers like mad after Dr. Spock has spoken is a co-conspirator . . . ? That is substantially correct, answered Mr. Wall.*

When defense attorneys asked for the names of those so counseled, the government referred them to the Census Bureau on the grounds that the publicity given by the news media to statements by the defendants had made every eligible draftee a possible counselee.

> John P. McKenzie, of the Washington *Post,* followed up on this . . . pretending grave concern for his own safety. He asked Wall: If the media are responsible for spreading the Spock message to the whole draft-age male population, is not a reporter who files a story about a demonstration . . . part of the conspiracy? Mr. Wall, now rattled, avoided a direct answer. There is "no intention," he said, of indicting the media men.†

The trial ended in acquittal for Raskin and conviction for the other four defendants. In July, 1969, the U.S. Court of Appeals overruled the verdicts, freeing Spock and Ferber and, curiously, ordering a retrial for Goodman and Coffin. In a dissenting opinion that held all four should have been freed, Judge Frank M. Coffin gave his opinion of the proceedings and the issues raised:

> This is a landmark case, and no one, I take it, supposes that this will be the last attempt by the government to use the conspiracy weapon. . . . The court's rationale provides no meaningful basis for predicting who will find themselves within the net. Finally, there is the greater danger that the casting of the net has scared away many whom the government has no right to catch.

Justice Coffin was quite right, of course. It was not by any means to be the last attempt by the government to use the conspiracy

---

* *Ibid.,* p. 71.
† *Ibid.*

weapon. Even as he wrote his opinion, the Justice Department of the Nixon Administration, picking up the baton left by the Johnson Administration, was proceeding with its case against the Chicago Eight, charged with conspiracy to cross state lines for the purpose of inciting riot in the Chicago convention melee of August, 1968, under a law passed in response to the ghetto violence of 1967. Aside from punishing the organizers of the Chicago demonstrations, the purpose of this trial seemed to be an attempt to tar all the various activist elements of the peace movement with the same brush, equating the radical but essentially pacifist element headed by Dave Dellinger with the less pacifistic Students for a Democratic Society (S.D.S.), represented by Rennie Davis and Tom Hayden, the volatile Yippies, represented by Abbie Hoffman, and the vanguard of militant black protest and resistance, represented in the person of Black Panther Bobby Seale. If the precedent of the "Boston Five" trial means anything, it implicates in addition all those who came to Chicago to demonstrate during that terrible August week, as well as the convention delegates who joined them. And might it not also implicate the press, which covered the violence and was charged with being biased toward the demonstrators?

If Agnew's Des Moines and Montgomery talks were efforts to discredit the press with "the great silent majority," the Chicago trial revealed a pattern of government behavior that has increasingly begun to discredit the press with the demonstrating minority. This is the increasing use of undercover agents who pose as reporters, including the duping of bona fide newsmen to serve unwittingly in such a role. One such was Sheldon Ramsdell, a thirty-four-year-old free-lance photographer and former press-aide for Senator Eugene McCarthy during the 1968 primaries. Ramsdell's story was related in James Wechsler's column in the New York *Post.* He had joined an organization that called itself the New York Press Service after the McCarthy effort was over. The hapless photographer learned of his true role when his employer, one Louis Salzberg, who established himself as a reporter by obtaining press credentials from a Spanish-language newspaper, testified at the Chicago trial that his "news" service was subsidized by the F.B.I., from which he had received a total of ten thousand dollars since 1967. The job he was paid for was to monitor the peace movement for the federal agency. Those who worked for him unknowingly served that same purpose. In his column Wechsler asked: "How many other journalists—TV and newspaper variety—are on the F.B.I. payroll?" It is a question seriously being asked throughout the peace movement and, indeed, by those involved in every form of dissident or protest activity. This is not to charge a deliberate effort on the part of government agencies to discredit the press with dissident elements, but it could hardly be more effective if it were deliberate. Nor is it hampered in any way by press reaction to the practice. With the exception of an occasional columnist, the press to date has been entirely passive in the face of widespread impersonation by federal and local police spies.

On the eve of the October 15 Moratorium against the war Vice President Agnew characterized its organizers as "effete snobs" and went on to observe that *Nhan Dan,* the official organ of the North Vietnamese Communist party, had published an open letter from that party congratulating the Moratorium and wishing its efforts well. Calling on the Moratorium leaders to disavow such support, Agnew called the letter an "incredible" intrusion into the internal affairs of the United States; he never mentioned the fact that the United States had bombed North Vietnam for three and a half years and had sent more than a half-million men into South Vietnam. The absurdity of that particular statement aside, Agnew's remark was only one of a series of charges, direct and indirect, made by Nixon officials and unofficial supporters that war protestors were helping the enemy and that those who urged a speedy end to the war were prolonging it by undercutting the Administration's position at the Paris talks—where negotiations were stalled at dead center and had been for months.

Undeterred by veiled and explicit charges of treason, the Moratorium organizers planned for the next step in their campaign, the Washington demonstration of November 15. Their efforts received added emphasis by Nixon's November 3 Vietnam speech, during which he disappointed the expectant and confirmed the cynical by saying absolutely nothing new and, in saying it, reviving the rhetorical distortions of the Johnson Administration, and by stating that he would not allow protests and demonstrations to affect him in any way. His speech greatly pleased the Thieu Government in Saigon, but it pushed over the line a large number of Americans who had theretofore been uncertain whether they should continue vocal and active opposition or give the President a chance. The press, of course, documented this effect and freely analyzed the contents (or the lack of same) of the address. The three television networks did so immediately following the live broadcast of the talk. At one point in his talk Nixon spoke of his efforts to break the Paris deadlock. He quoted a letter he had personally sent to Ho Chi Minh (which said nothing of substance beyond a repetition of his desire to negotiate "an early resolution of this tragic war") and then stated that Ho Chi Minh's reply had been a "flat rejection" of his "initiative." Marvin Kalb, participating in CBS's post-address analysis, disagreed, finding significant differences in text and tone from previous North Vietnamese responses. Nixon, Kalb seemed to feel (along with many students of the situation), may have missed a signal. In any event, the consensus of network commentary, if such it can be called, was largely critical and negative, if only because no analyst could point to anything new in a long-awaited and long and widely heralded speech—with the one possible exception of the coinage of the "silent majority" slogan.

Following the address, and as the planned antiwar demonstration in Washington gathered steam, Attorney General John N. Mitchell and the Justice Department began to sound dire warnings of widespread violence and bloodshed when the marchers arrived. To those who wanted to demonstrate in the nation's capital, these warnings seemed an all too transparent effort to frighten people away from the affair and soften, if not extinguish, its political impact. To others it seemed possible that the Attorney General might have been preparing the ground for officially initiated violence *à la* Chicago. The press, along with a number of Congressmen and private citizens, called attention to these developments and warned about the possibility that the government's attitude and actions were creating a tension that might well lead to the self-fulfillment of its own prophecy. The chief bone of contention concerned the parade route, the government at first refusing to permit the marchers access to Pennsylvania Avenue. Ultimately, a compromise was reached, and the demonstrators were able to use much of the avenue for their march. The demonstration was the largest the city had ever experienced, and what violence did occur was meager and confined to a small group of movement apaches in front of the Justice Department. None of the fifty thousand soldiers and paratroopers called into the city for the occasion by a nervous Administration were needed. The affair was a huge success.

Most of the demonstrators were elated at the outcome, but there was mounting evidence that the Nixon Administration remained highly displeased. Mitchell even seemed displeased that major violence had not occurred, and adding weight to the argument of those who felt he had been trying to provoke violence to discredit the demonstration, he insisted on characterizing it the following day as having been violent—and gave all the credit for the fact that it was not the beginning of the Revolution to the Army and the Washington, D.C., police. He also charged the demonstration's parade marshals with bad faith in not preventing the little fracas before the Justice Department (though they had successfully controlled more than 250,000 people along the line of march!). An insight into the Attorney General's attitude toward the whole affair, and the peace movement in general, was offered by his wife in the course of a CBS interview on November 20. "My husband made the comment to me, looking out the Justice Department, that it looked like the Russian Revolution going on." During the same interview Mrs. Mitchell quoted her husband as having opined many times that "some of the liberals in this country, he'd like to take them and change them for Russian Communists."

The Nixon Administration seemed generally displeased—displeased with the reception of the media to his speech, displeased with the media's treatment of his critics (and, in particular, the two Moratorium activities), and displeased with the success of the Washington demonstration. On November 13, two days prior to the march, Spiro T. Agnew had flown to Des Moines to deliver his now famous critique of the networks. The week following the march he flew to Montgomery, Alabama, George Wallace's backyard, to attack *The New York Times,* the Washington *Post,* and the "liberal" printed press in general. One cannot help but speculate about the timing of those two speeches and wonder whether or not advance intelligence as to the numbers of people likely to come to Washington on November 15 might not have decided the first attack on those the Administration held responsible for publicizing the march. One also wonders whether the obvious success of the march might not have affected the decision to broaden the attack in the second speech. That this issue was of major importance in the Des Moines address is obvious: "We cannot measure this power and influence by the traditional democratic standards," said the Vice President, "for these men can create national issues overnight. *They can make or break by their coverage and commentary a moratorium on the war* [my italics]." What seems to have been signaled by the November Offensive, whatever else it may portend, is that the Nixon Administration has expanded its attack on active dissent from the actual dissenters and their leaders to the dissenters' use of the nation's communications channels and those who permit such use. (By "use" I do not mean manipulation, but simply access: the ability of organized groups of Americans to tell the rest of the country what they think and what they are doing.) By Agnew's logic, it was the networks who were primarily responsible for a quarter-million people showing up in Washington on November 15.

The increasing proclivity of government to manipulate the information the public receives, to screen it through the filters of policy, and to advance its ability to control the shape of public opinion have been discussed earlier, as well as various conflicts between the government and the press, the latter resisting the former in a struggle to preserve its role as an independent source of information and as a representative of the people's right to know. The November Offensive was yet another struggle in this continuing conflict, an escalation definitely, but another battle following many others that have occurred in the Information War. In his Des Moines speech Agnew pointedly stated his main concern, and that of the Administration, by attacking the handling of Nixon's November 3 address:

When Winston Churchill rallied public opinion to stay the course against Hitler's Germany, he didn't have to contend with a gaggle of commentators raising doubts about whether he was reading public opinion right, or whether Britain had the stamina to see the war through. [It might be noted that Hitler had no such "gaggle of commentators" to contend with either.]

His main concern was also made obvious by what must be read as a significant repetition: Toward the middle of his remarks, referring to a TV commentator's skeptical comments on the dependability of Nixon's campaign promises, Agnew said,

> But this attack emanated from the privileged sanctuary of a network studio and therefore had the apparent dignity of an objective statement. *The American people would rightly not tolerate this concentration of power in government* [my italics].

At the end of his speech, after returning to the issue of network commentators supplying critical analyses of the President's Vietnam-policy address, the Vice President repeated,

> Now, my friends, we'd never trust such power as I've described over public opinion in the hands of an elected government.

Many commentators and columnists have pointed out the implicit threats of the Des Moines speech in such phrasing as: "perhaps it is time that the networks were *made* more responsive to the views of the nation [my italics]," "whether or not the networks have *abused* the power they enjoy [my italics]," and "the networks have claimed a First Amendment right to the same unlimited freedoms held by the great newspapers of America. But the situations are not identical." Most of the comment on these remarks has pointed to the implied threat of the use of federal licensing power to whip television news into line. Without wanting to sound the shrill trumpet of paranoia, I submit there is another aspect to the speech that merits awareness if not concern. That is the question, "How many marches and demonstrations would we have if the marchers did not know that the ever-faithful TV cameras would be there to record their antics for the next news show?," placed in the context of the Spock trial and the increasing use by the government of the conspiracy weapon. Might that same weapon conceivably be used one day against "a tiny, enclosed fraternity of privileged men elected by no one and enjoying a monopoly sanctioned and licensed by government"? One doubts very seriously that such a thought ever occurred to the Vice President, but that does not mean that its seed may not rest snug and warm in some dark place in the Nixon Administration's attitude toward dissent and the media.

There were a number of absurdities and misstatements of fact in that Des Moines talk, but none more absurd than the implication that the government has too little power to influence public opinion. It is this writer's view that it has dangerously too much and that present policy seems to be a concerted effort at further aggrandizement. In its effort to discredit the news media, the Nixon Administration seems, at least temporarily, to have pulled out all the stops, employing provincial prejudice, generational antagonisms, and divisions over the Vietnam war. It also employed some hard truths. In his co-optation of the liberal critique of the media Agnew struck at some very sensitive spots that cannot be altogether argued away by observations, however valid, concerning the Vice President's (or the Administration's) true purposes.

■ CHAPTER 9 ■

The Enemy Within

*The stifling weight of censorship is to be found not in the
hearing rooms of the Federal Communications Commission,
but in the conference rooms of this nation's largest television
networks.*
—Nicholas Johnson, F.C.C. Commissioner

The above comment, made in a separate but concurring statement in the F.C.C.'s decision to dismiss complaints against WBAI-
FM concerning the broadcast of anti-Semitic remarks, referred
specifically to CBS's cancellation of the "Smothers Brothers Comedy Hour." In the same statement the commissioner echoed William Henry's speech to the National Association of Broadcasters
nearly five years before, charging the broadcasting industry with
an "ignominious silence" in defense of free speech and for being
dedicated to "free speech for profit only." The repetition of that
observation, particularly by a member of the Federal Communications Commission, uncovers an anomaly central to the relationship
of government and press, and especially between government and
broadcasting, and underlines a profoundly important truth: Some
of the most serious dangers to the institution of the free press lie
within that institution itself.

At least until the November Offensive, the *overt* pressures for
censorship and repression which had arisen from government had
been rather tentative and weak, Senator Pastore notwithstanding.
For long the truly disturbing thing about the situation has been the
failure of the press, and especially the electronic press, to meet even

those attacks on the First Amendment with anything like concerted forcefulness. Even with the fairly strong reaction to Agnew's attack, one wonders how long such principled resistance will hold up. Walter Cronkite, when asked if he thought the industry had over-reacted to Agnew, replied that if anything, he felt it had not reacted strongly enough. Others in the television medium have privately expressed fears that the brave front might crumble. A key element in the Administration's charges against the press, and particularly against network television, is that it is too uniformly "liberal" (Chet Huntley, Eric Sevareid, and ABC too liberal?). With the subsidence of at least the first wave of the offensive begun in November, after having made an apparently successful effort to turn the "silent majority" into phone-callers and letter-writers, after having adopted a somewhat lower profile that does not force network executives to defend publicly their honor and the integrity of their news operations, the Administration might wisely wait a while to see if the front continues to hold.

One significant result of the offensive seems to have been the movement of the political reference point considerably to the Right, at least in the minds of much of the public. Certainly that has occurred in the Administration's rhetoric and would seem to be one of its principal goals (perhaps it was deemed necessary in order to get the rest of Richard Nixon—the "old" Nixon—comfortably inside). That is the clear effect of turning Sevareid and Huntley into liberals, and of balancing the John Birch Society on the Right with Americans for Democratic Action on the Left, as U.S.I.A. Director Frank Shakespeare (a former CBS executive) did at a gathering of television newsmen in Detroit scarcely six weeks before Agnew's Des Moines speech.* It may be the critical thing to watch:

* In all fairness I must confess that I found most of Shakespeare's *specific* criticisms of television handling of news stories well taken. Speaking before the annual Paul White Awards dinner of the Radio-Television News Directors Association on September 26, he referred specifically to the treatment of three news stories: (1) the 1964 Republican convention in San Francisco, where the networks drummed up a false drama by reporting William Scranton, of Pennsylvania, as a serious contender for the Presidential nomination when it was clear that Goldwater had it all locked up from the beginning; (2) the 1968 Republican convention in Miami, where the networks touted Nelson Rockefeller, of New York, as serious competition for Richard Nixon, whose only possible competition was California's

whether or not the networks, while ostensibly sustaining their resistance to government pressure, adopt a similar shift in orientation of the political spectrum. (If Chet Huntley and Howard K. Smith are liberals, should David Brinkley and Walter Cronkite send their résumés to *Pravda?*) Often in the past it has seemed that the reaction to demands for self-censorship was to denounce the demands and then to acquiesce in them.

CBS denounced Pastore's demand for prior screening of programs by the N.A.B. and then, within a week, abruptly canceled the principal target of Pastore's criticism within its control—the Smothers brothers. On the other hand, it is the opinion of Nicholas Johnson (and of many in Washington and elsewhere) that the broadcasting industry in general and the networks in particular are currently so powerful as to defy control by anyone and are "beyond the check of any institution in our society."*

Glaring as the contradiction seems, there are reasons that resolve it. One is that the broadcasting industry's "courage" (i.e., concern) in the area of program integrity and independence does not match its power. It is, after all, an *industry*. To state that it is more concerned with its balance sheets than with the issues of free speech and free press is not to indulge in sarcasm but merely to observe a fact. Nor is it the only industry more concerned with the

---

Ronald Reagan; and (3) the story of the platoon from the Americal Division in Vietnam which refused to move out. Shakespeare charged that in the last case the networks indicated the refusal as a political act and a vote against the war. I don't personally recall gathering that impression from network stories at the time, but if he is correct, then the impression given was quite wrong: It was a common case of fear, exhaustion, and a subsequent failure of will, according to all I heard and read and according to my own knowledge of what is likely in the circumstances. In saying that, however, I profoundly disagree with the point these examples were supposed to document, that these failures are simply attributable to the fact that most television newsmen covering and commenting on the stories were liberals. They were professional, not political, failures, and if that distinction cannot be maintained, then we might as well return to the era when press organizations were simply the organs of political parties.

I would also agree with his suggestion that the answer to the problem is to include more representatives of other political persuasions if he had not moved the center of the political spectrum so far to the Right and then suggested the inclusion only of conservatives.

* "The Whole World Is Watching," Public Broadcast Laboratory documentary, 1968.

margin of its profits than with the quality of its product. Whatever the rhetoric used, the cardinal principle of broadcasting is not free speech or communication but free enterprise, and this provides another reason for the seeming contradiction.

In addition to its own power to influence the public, the industry has an effective weapon at hand with which to fight off governmental incursions into program and news content—the First Amendment to the Constitution. On the other hand, there is no First Amendment for economic activities, these being long established as legitimately subject to regulation and control by the government. Furthermore, certain varieties of speech have, along with obscenity, been generally excluded from the broad-gauge protection of the First Amendment, e.g., fraudulent advertising. Legally vulnerable, then, at the heart of its operation—its true *raison d'être*—the industry has been less than sanguine about defending secondary principles, especially when such defense is likely to anger those in Congress or in the F.C.C. who are technically empowered to affect the important things in the industry's life. Thus, every effort was made to pull the First Amendment blanket over economic activities (commercials), even if it means leaving bare such peripheral concerns as news, opinion, comedy, and satire. This is the phenomenon William Henry accurately described when he denounced the double standard of the industry toward free speech during the 1963 Pacific investigations. The aptness of Johnson's statement about the great power of the industry was also evidenced at that time, for the F.C.C. was able to harass Pacifica while the industry was silent, but it was unable to limit commercial time and frequency due to the congressional lobbying of an aroused industry brandishing the First Amendment! But never has the situation been quite so succinctly exposed and articulated as by the *quid pro quo* offered the broadcasters by Senator Pastore at the 1969 N.A.B. convention: If they would set up an industry-wide censorship bureau, he would bend his considerable efforts and influence to calling off the F.C.C.'s dogs in the economic arena.

Robert MacNeil, former NBC correspondent, author of *The People Machine,* and moderator for the Public Broadcast Laboratory's "The Whole World Is Watching," asked in his concluding remarks on that program:

> If broadcasting, as it repeatedly claims, feels entitled to the protection given to newspapers under the First Amendment, why doesn't it force a court test of that right? If it is inappropriate, as CBS President Frank Stanton told the violence commission on Friday, for any governmental body to raise questions involving news judgments, why does he not refuse to cooperate?

These questions are particularly pertinent, because the course they suggest for the industry might limit the proliferation of self-censorship that afflicts it today and which is, both in the electronic and in the print media, one of the greatest weaknesses of contemporary American journalism and one of the greatest dangers to the institution of a truly free press. In some significant respects "voluntary" censorship is more damaging and dangerous, because more pervasive and insidious, than overt government control and the imposition of prior censorship. To use an extreme example, there was at least a kind of brutal honesty in the glaring white spaces in Saigon's newspapers before censorship was "abolished." It was obvious that an item had been deleted by the government censor; the reader was fully aware that this or that story was incomplete, possibly in its most significant aspects, and generally aware that he was not getting all the news and quite possibly not the most important news; and the newspaper and its staff were thus allowed to maintain, if they so chose, a certain dignity and professional integrity.

An altogether different situation emerges when, as it did in Saigon, censorship does not diminish but simply becomes less open, when every newspaper operates by anticipating governmental action against it, not only for content but also for tone and editorial direction. In this respect, one of the most significant closings of Saigon newspapers since the "end" of censorship was the suspension of the Saigon *Daily News,* an English-language paper. The *News* was closed because it did not display a government announcement with sufficient prominence! Under the "voluntary" system the government exercises positive as well as negative control, and the integrity and credibility of the press is almost totally destroyed—though "credibility" may return when the public is sufficiently brainwashed.

Such an analogy may seem a gross exaggeration of any possible dangers facing the American scene to those who have forgotten the effects of McCarthyism on broadcasting, a dismaying and dishonorable slice of recent history: the system of blacklisting in radio and television; the activities of organizations such as the American Legion, AWARE, ALERT, and of publications such as *Red Channels* and *Counterattack,* which circulated lists of names to network executives; and the almost unbelievably craven acquiescence of the networks. Hundreds of talented and experienced newsmen, as well as actors and writers, were forced out of broadcasting as a result of private charges—and as a result of the charges alone, charges with little or no substantiation. Worse, such substantiation was rarely asked for. Self-censorship, not only to protect one's current job but also to protect one's very ability to work in the profession, became the order of the day. Programs of a genuinely controversial nature were strictly avoided, particularly programs in the realm of politics and foreign relations. What, for instance, could a CBS reporter (who wanted to remain with CBS or even remain a reporter) have done at that time with a story critical of the American Legion or with an exposé of AWARE? Reporters and newscasters watched what they said and how they phrased the questions they asked, and if they didn't, their superiors did. Editors and producers were conscious of the threat in the assignments they gave and in the stories they used. There seems little question but that the dismal showing of the American press during the Korean War was, to a significant degree, the result of this atmosphere.

The scars of that period, at least in broadcasting, have not disappeared to this day. Many of those who were responsible for the industry's surrender of every principle that justified its existence outside of the profit motive are still in leadership positions today. A number of actors and performers blacklisted at the time still find it difficult or impossible to appear on the networks—the folk singer Pete Seeger being probably the best-known example. But the scars and aftereffects of blacklisting in broadcasting are most significantly evident in certain biases and imbalances in programming, both news and entertainment, dealing with or encroaching on areas of political controversy. The Smothers brothers were both criticized and censored by CBS (prior to the cancellation of their show) for expressing decidedly partisan views against the Vietnam war. And yet there is no public evidence that the Vietnam "entertainment" shows of comedian Bob Hope, now an annual television event liberally sprinkled with hawkish jokes, skits, comments, and cracks about opponents of the war, have ever drawn similar network fire. They certainly, at this writing, have not been deleted. Robert MacNeil, in *The People Machine,* pointed to a similar imbalance among television newscasters. There was, he said, little doubt in the minds of those who listened regularly to NBC's Huntley-Brinkley team that Chet Huntley tended to be hawkish on the subject and felt little compunction about letting that fact come through on his newscasts. The knowledge that David Brinkley is something of a dove, on the other hand, was long limited to those who knew him personally. Again, one wonders what the effect of the November Offensive will be on that situation, and wondering, one fears it cannot greatly improve it.

Monopoly and Conglomeration

Long before Spiro Agnew, Nat Hentoff remarked that the main thing wrong with *The New York Times* these days is the absence of the New York *Herald Tribune.* These two papers, he felt, not only provided the city with a greater variety of morning news but also tended to keep one another honest and hard-working. After the merger of the *Tribune* with the *World-Telegram & Sun* and the *Journal-American* and the subsequent demise of the whole ungainly mess in 1967, the *Times* was left with only the *Daily News* and the *Post* for competition, neither of which can pretend to compete with the *Times* either in terms of the scope of their coverage or in professional quality and influence (even though, according to a 1967 survey, the circulation of the *Daily News* exceeds that of the *Times* by nearly half a million). Hentoff was pointing out a local effect of one of the most serious dangers to American journalism and the people's right to know: the progressive reduction of sources through economic attrition and cannibalism.

In his excellent study, *The First Freedom,* Bryce W. Rucker detailed the decline of American newspapers. In New York City at the beginning of the century fifteen general-circulation metropolitan dailies competed with one another. Today there are three. Nationally, 2,600 daily newspapers were in operation in 1909. Today the number is less by nearly a thousand. Even that loss is a misleading index of the decline, Rucker points out, because of the significant increase in population between then and now and a simultaneous decrease in illiteracy, and the trend toward "monopoly newspaper cities":

> In 1910, 57.1 per cent of the daily-newspaper towns were served by more than one newspaper ownership; within a decade the percentage declined to 42.7. By 1930 an alarming deterioration had set in; only in 21.5 per cent of the daily-newspaper cities did readers have access to competing dailies. The erosion has continued, and we find that by mid-1967 only in 64 of 1,547 American daily-newspaper cities (4.13 per cent) did commercial dailies compete. The rate of decline . . . still is quite high.

Chain take-overs and the trend toward multi-media ownership (newspaper ownership of broadcasting outlets, etc.) have further diminished the variety of news and opinion sources available to the American people. Rucker found that while the number of newspapers has declined since the early part of the century, the number of newspapers owned by chains has increased. The squeeze is made still tighter by the increasing reliance of newspapers upon syndicated feature service and the wire services for much of their daily content.

Radio and television have exhibited the same trend, but with a vengeance, as in the case of Boston's WHDH-TV, owned by a newspaper (the Boston *Herald Traveler*) and affiliated with a network (CBS). The nature of communications monopolies or near monopolies is indicated by a complaint filed with the F.C.C. in July, 1969, by Milton J. Schapp, a Pennsylvania millionaire and former Democratic gubernatorial candidate. Schapp asked the F.C.C. to reject the license-renewal application of Philadelphia's WFIL-TV. The television station, an affiliate of ABC, is owned by the communications combine of Walter H. Annenberg (who is the Nixon Administration's new ambassador to London). The Annenberg empire includes Philadelphia's only morning newspaper, the Philadelphia *Inquirer,* the Philadelphia *Daily News,* WFIL-TV, WFIL-AM, WFIL-FM, three other television stations covering the Pennsylvania area, as well as the popular magazine *TV Guide.* Annenberg was also the largest single stockholder in the Pennsylvania Railroad and is currently a director of its successor company, Penn Central Transportation. Part of the Schapp complaint alleged that Annenberg's *Inquirer* had endorsed the merger of the Pennsylvania Railroad with the New York Central and that Annenberg had then turned the full might of his communications empire against Schapp's election bid after the latter opposed the merger.*

The networks have dominated programming in broadcasting (especially television programming) to an alarming extent. The network concept is of crucial importance to broadcasting, particularly to broadcast news. No individual radio or television station, no matter how large an audience or successful an advertising base it can boast, can support the costs of a national (not to mention international) news operation. Given the level of expense in broadcasting, only some form of network arrangement can possibly provide a sufficient financial base for such an operation. The need for diversity and local independence, however, is at least of equal importance. In the relatively short history of American broadcasting the numerous small and medium-sized networks have been progressively slain or swallowed up by bigger fish, until today the nation is served by only six radio and television networks, the format and content of whose news and public-affairs programming, to make matters worse, is so nearly identical as to be interchangeable. Although outright network ownership of stations is limited,

* *The New York Times,* July 4, 1969.

the limitation is more apparent than real. CBS owns only five television stations, but they serve the five major metropolitan areas of the nation. In addition, each network dominates prime-time programming on their many affiliate stations. Below the level of network operations there is the widespread practice of group ownership: The same company owns a number of individual radio or television stations scattered throughout a region or across the country. In an article entitled "The American Media Baronies" in the July, 1969, issue of *The Atlantic Monthly* the editors discussed the implications of the trend:

> Group ownership means, by definition, that few stations in major markets will be locally owned. . . . But the basic point is simply that the national political power involved in owner-ship of a group of major VHF television stations in, say, New York, Los Angeles, Philadelphia, and Washington, D.C., is greater than a democracy should unthinkingly repose in one man or corporation.

Another major example of the potentially lethal impact of big-business trends on modern-day journalism is the growth of con-glomerates. Conglomeration, in the economic world, is the owner-ship and control, under a single corporate roof, of many disparate and mostly unrelated businesses and industries. Monopoly, the classic method of industrial and mercantile accretion whereby one railroad buys up all the other railroads (along with the coal, oil, steel, and lumber necessary for their construction and mainte-nance), has long been restricted (more or less) by antitrust legisla-tion. Conglomeration, although subject to governmental regulation and control, is hardly restricted, and today it accounts for a massive concentration of the nation's economic and industrial resources which would have made the unchecked monopolists and robber barons of the nineteenth century green with envy. The potential effect of this trend on the institution of the free press is far more serious than that of simple monopoly. The trend toward press monopoly threatens the number of independent sources and out-lets; the ultimate result of this trend, carried to its logical extreme, might be the Orwellian specter of a single national newspaper and a single radio-television network, one of them owning the other. Conglomeration, on the other hand, threatens the independence of the press as *a function*—not just the independence of press outlets—in the subordination of news and broadcasting organizations to the interests of steel, oil, automobiles, missile parts, or whatever else constitutes the *major* investments of the conglomerate's parent.

Consider the present case of the Radio Corporation of America. RCA, which formed NBC in 1926, is one of the largest manufacturers of electronic parts and gadgetry in the nation. It is also one of the largest defense contractors and is involved in the development and production of ballistic missiles and the early-warning system. RCA can scarcely be expected to be unconcerned with such questions as defense spending and the ABM controversy. In addition, the RCA conglomerate purchased Random House, Inc., the publishing company, in 1966, which had previously swallowed up Alfred A. Knopf, Inc. Potentially, the interests and judgment of the publishers are subordinate to the interests of both the broadcasters and the makers of missile parts. (CBS similarly branched out to acquire Holt, Rinehart and Winston, Inc.)

CBS and ABC still own themselves—though ABC remains independent through no fault of its own. In 1967 a merger of ABC with the giant International Telephone and Telegraph Corporation was approved by the F.C.C., in spite of a host of serious questions raised about the effect such a merger would have on the network's independence in news programming. I.T.T. is both a major defense contractor (40 per cent of its domestic income, according to Rucker) and a huge international business empire (60 per cent of its total income). What effect might this have on ABC's international news operations, particularly in countries and on issues close to the founts of I.T.T.'s income? Predictably, the I.T.T. replied, "None." Even if that were true at the time—which is to say, even if the current directors of I.T.T., being men of goodwill, intended to keep "hands off" ABC programming—to permit such a situation to develop would have been grossly irresponsible. Any system that grants such power on the basis of "goodwill" and the promise of the recipient not to use it doesn't ask for disaster, it demands it! But that is precisely what the F.C.C. did. As to the validity of that promise—the reality of that goodwill—Rucker has the following to say:

> Three reporters who were covering the [F.C.C.] hearings—Miss Eileen Shanahan, *New York Times;* Jed Stout, United Press International; and Stephen M. Aug, Associated Press—testified that I.T.T. press officials had attempted to influence their stories, both by applying pressure on them and through their superiors. What more evidence did commissioners committed to the merger need to counter pious promises by I.T.T. officials that they would not interfere in ABC news decisions?

Fortunately, the Justice Department was not so pliant or so gullible as the F.C.C. on this issue, and in the face of increasing unhappiness on the part of that department I.T.T. subsequently dropped the merger. But even for the two networks that remain independent of larger corporate empires there is still the serious question posed by their own initiation of conglomerate activities. To what extent do their activities in separate fields tend to decrease the *real* independence of their broadcast activities, and especially of their news and public-affairs operations? The evidence is far from reassuring. Those in charge of all three major networks and of many smaller radio and television chains are business men responsible for a large, composite, profit-making machine, of which news operations are only small and not terribly profitable parts. In his book, *Television and the News,* Harry J. Skornia, a professor of radio and television at the University of Illinois, makes the following observation:

> Since the controllers of the broadcast media, generally, represent corporate and business orientations, and find the present broadcasting and economic systems profitable, they have a special stake in the continuation of the present situation. They therefore view as disruptive, radical, subversive, or even unpatriotic, forces, materials, and programs which might, however indirectly, disrupt the present arrangement. It is natural that the voices of these media should speak the language of business, for their masters are big business, and there are many things about which they would prefer to keep the people of America quiet and uncritical.

Many writers have commented on—and at least one psychological experiment was conducted to explore—the manner and effectiveness with which the attitudes and predilections of "the boss" or
the company are assimilated and incorporated by subordinates in
the news profession. This, of course, is a basic human failing. It
therefore becomes especially destructive in journalism when the
people at the top are not steeped in and dedicated to the principles
of that profession but rather to corporate profit-and-loss columns,
the arithmetic of which may be radically affected by whether or not
the American people feel they need a large standing army or an
antiballistic-missile defense system.

Media monopoly, multiple ownership, and conglomeration have
been receiving increasing attention lately, both from Congress and
from federal agencies, including the F.C.C. The record is mixed,
however. The so-called failing-newspaper bill is still, at this writing,
pending in Congress. The bill, if enacted, would permit newspapers
in a single city to combine operations and enter into agreements as
to advertising rates, circulation competition, etc—agreements that,
without such a bill, would make them liable under existing antitrust
legislation. The bill is being strongly supported by Congressmen
with interests in the newspaper business who also want a section of
the bill which requires demonstration of "failing" on the part of one
of the newspapers to be deleted. The Federal Communications
Commission has made some effort recently to increase diversity, to
widen access to the airwaves, and to defend news and opinion from
censorship and suppression by the industry itself, but in the
opinion of many students of the media the commission has been all
too timid in pursuing these purposes. The facts are that diversity is
shrinking, access to the media is more difficult, and censorship is as
great (in some respects greater) as it has ever been. Long considered little more than a water boy for the industry, the F.C.C.
scarcely improved its image with its actions in the I.T.T.–ABC
merger case. The strange alliance between the repressive attitudes
of congressional yahoos and federal bureaucrats on the one hand
and the profit-sensitivity of the network censors on the other has
increasingly thwarted the timorous efforts of a federal regulatory
agency to nourish and protect the thin wraith of the First Amend-

ment in broadcasting. That alliance, the most wondrous thing to behold since the Hitler-Stalin pact, could never have been more starkly dramatized than it was in the Pastore deal.

The broadcast journalist is caught in the middle of this squeeze, and he knows it well. Many of them admit privately that there are vital subjects they do not go near and far-from-vital subjects that receive coverage because of extrajournalistic considerations. News stories and documentaries are not infrequently slanted in the direction of the commercial interests of the networks and their advertisers, and sometimes wholly inspired by such interests. One example was the general tone of news and documentary coverage of pay TV (largely negative), which goes against the economic grain of an industry based on advertising. Another was an essentially frivolous documentary broadcast by ABC entitled "Blondes Have More Fun," a program sponsored by the hair-coloring firm Clairol, whose ads feature the same assertion. That probing, hard-hitting documentary found, as its title indicates, that blondes *do* have more fun. It is not the kind of performance calculated to win public trust and confidence. Similarly, both NBC and CBS, along with a large number of major newspapers that have large advertising accounts with the tobacco industry, managed to report the death from lung cancer of actor Robert Taylor without mentioning that he smoked three packs of cigarettes a day since childhood—a significant fact given prominent attention in both the U.P.I and A.P. wire-service accounts,* from which both newspapers and the networks usually learn of such stories.

In his separate but concurring statement in the case of the U.F.T. vs. WBAI, Commissioner Johnson quoted the following line from the 1969 *Cornell Law Review* dealing with the same subject: "When the private sector turns censor, it is time to trust the public." Although that opinion may one day be interred among the "famous last words" of contemporary democracy, many dedicated friends of the free press and the First Amendment feel there is little reason to argue with it today, because, quite simply, there seems so little recourse.

* *Straus Editor's Report,* June 13, 1969.

Commercialism, Show-Biz, and the News

The commercial nature of news-gathering organizations (that is, that they are profit-seeking enterprises in competition with other profit-seeking enterprises) has always affected the performance of professional journalism, and the competition of the marketplace has been both constructive and harmful. Such competition affected both content and style, the kind of format, and the scope and depth of coverage of newspapers and magazines long before broadcasting ever appeared on the scene. Most intelligent newspaper readers are aware of the competition of bright, flashy headlines to catch the eye of the passerby, even though the sense of the headline often distorts the content of the story it advertises (a practice that becomes greatly intensified when two or more competing newspapers in the same city run the same story from the same source, usually a wire service or feature syndicate). Most readers are also aware, on the other hand, of the value of having access to more than one journalistic version of an event, a luxury available only to those in areas where two or more newspapers compete.

In broadcasting, particularly television, there is an added and highly unfortunate dimension to traditional competition. Not only do the networks and individual stations compete with one another, but the news and public-affairs sections of each are forced into an entirely unfair competition with the balance—the great bulk—of the outlet's programming: entertainment. The contest is for air time and the arbiter is the ratings, and in the contest the standards of journalism and show-biz collide, usually with the former losing. As Skornia points out, the standards of responsible journalism would interpret low ratings in a given news area as a probable indicator of public ignorance and disinterest in that area and a challenge to newsmen to communicate its importance to the listener or viewer and create an interest. By the standards of commercial show-biz, however, "low ratings are generally used either to cause or to rationalize dropping or de-emphasizing whatever is rated." The rhetoric for this practice, of course, is "giving people what they want." Skornia adds, quite rightly, that "to select news on the basis of 'what the people want,' or ratings, or any extraneous value is to destroy the meaning of news."

The old song "There's No Business like Show Business" is something of an overstatement. Broadcast news is, in all too many respects, very much like show business. It is dominated by the star system and the ratings, television's answer to the box office. It emphasizes drama and pace over content and depth; it pushes interest at the expense of understanding; it overemphasizes the importance of picture and underrates the importance of information. Show-biz, in its very soul, has always been contemptuous of art, and it is no less so of journalism.

The show-biz mentality of television journalism is nowhere quite so evident as in the case of the "anchor men" of the network evening news programs. These men are chosen less for their professional competence as journalists (though they are often competent, and in some cases even talented, journalists) than for their ability to draw at the box office—their ratings. The dynamics of this kind of image consciousness and "audience response" are identical with those of show business, which notoriously selects for leading female roles not the actress with the greatest dramatic ability but the one with the greatest mammary glands. NBC and CBS have both settled, for the time being, on proven winners—Huntley-Brinkley in the one case, and Walter Cronkite in the other. ABC, on the other hand, always the poor stepsister in the network field, constantly struggling and experimenting to increase its ratings and its revenues, has gone through competent and qualified journalists (even a few highly talented ones) like a satyr through a whorehouse.

Some will answer that a certain photogenic quality and the ability to project an authoritative (sometimes avuncular) image are simply the broadcasting equivalents of literary style in the print media. This, I think, is a false analogy. Does James Reston have a *style?* If so, I would hate to be the one assigned to classify it. Reston's reputation is based rather on the cogency of his thought (when it is *cogent*) and on his genuine reportorial abilities. Tom Wicker is no great prose artist, but *The New York Times* values

him, rightly, because he is one of the more sensitive, talented
journalists working today, and because he is highly respected
among the more intelligent of the nation's newspaper readers.
Television's superstars owe their jobs far more to charisma than to
professional competence, and the two values simply are not comparable. Discussing television documentaries in *The People
Machine,* Robert MacNeil underlined this point when he asserted
that "on television the name and the face are still more important
than high journalistic standards." The insight MacNeil provides
into this process is worth repeating:

> To make a documentary appealing to the audience, the network
> will put its biggest news name on the program. The biggest
> names cannot afford to spend a month or six weeks away from
> their regular appearances in front of the studio cameras and
> the networks cannot spare them. So a high percentage of net-
> work documentaries are made by a producer, with a writer who
> is often the same man. When it is finished, the name commenta-
> tor is handed the completed script and he spends an hour re-
> cording it. To lend this exercise a little more authenticity, he
> may actually travel to a location and stay there just long enough
> to record a few pieces with his face on camera.

The contribution, then, of the superstar narrator is most often
limited to the use of his face and voice and the authority that they
impart, and the story itself is the creation of someone the audience
has never heard of. An interesting and valuable study might be
made contrasting audience reaction to a documentary narrated by
David Brinkley with audience reaction to the identical program
forced to stand on its own feet, *sans* Brinkley. At any rate, general
knowledge of the practice might resolve a few questions for those
who have been astonished and confounded by the seemingly tireless
ubiquity of men like Huntley and Cronkite. It might also act to
dispel the sense given by the television news story (for what is true
of the documentary is basically true of the evening news script)—a
sense intensified by the cryptic brevity of most television news
stories—that three sentences on Vietnam constitute the sufficient

word of God, chiseled on electronic tablets and brought down the mountain by a schizophrenic Moses.

Probably the most dramatic and extreme example of show-business practices in television news has gotten a good deal of attention, particularly since Chicago: the practice of "staging," manufacturing a scene in order to film it or, as is sometimes the case, stage-managing a genuine scene in progress or about to take place in order to make a better film story. In the latter respect there is an old story out of Vietnam, probably apocryphal, about a television crew covering a delta battle in which tanks were used. The tanks, advancing toward the enemy across open paddy fields, were spread widely in a standard attack formation. The TV correspondent walked over to the Vietnamese commander and asked blithely, "Colonel, could you please move your tanks in a little closer? I can't get them all in my picture."

According to *The New York Times* of March 2, 1969, the F.C.C., although clearing the networks of "bias" charges stemming from the Democratic convention in Chicago, "is still investigating four alleged examples of 'staged' incidents." These involve: (1) a "girl hippy" with a bandaged forehead who walked up to National Guard troops and shouted "Don't hit me!" when a filming crew gave her a cue; (2) a fire set by "what appeared to be a newsman" into which he put a "Welcome to Chicago" sign, which cameramen then photographed as it burned; (3) a camera crew that apparently asked a young man in Grant Park to hold a bandage to his head while they shot film, although he had no visible injury; (4) filming in Lincoln Park of a young man lying on the ground, being aided by girls in "white medical smocks," who later got up and talked to the crew without apparent injury.

There are different forms and degrees of staging, from the totally indefensible full production in the first example above to the essentially innocent, which the fourth example could have been if it were used and identified as an exercise demonstrating the first-aid techniques and medical preparedness of the demonstrators. Most staging acts fall somewhere in between and are essentially re-creations of what the correspondent or cameraman believes has happened. When a newspaper or magazine reporter arrives on the scene of a story too late to witness it himself, or if he misses important parts of it, he usually picks up the essentials from his colleagues. If a TV crew arrives on the scene late, they simply have no story; for them the essence of the story is its picture. With the pressure on, a crew will sometimes give in to the temptation to fake it, which may get them off the hook if they don't get caught. It is a temptation that sometimes becomes acute when the late crew arrives to find the competition with the story already in the can.

One staging incident I personally witnessed will always stick in my mind, not because the staging itself was so exceptional but because the cost was so high. It occurred in Feburary, 1968, in Hue during the month-long battle for the old Imperial City. I was at the rear headquarters of the First Battalion of the Fifth Marines; also present was a network television crew. The front lines were two blocks in front of us, and at the time the Marines were making another effort to advance. Across the road behind us was one of the battalion's companies; mauled and exhausted by days of bitter house-to-house fighting, it had been placed in temporary reserve. The television crew, old Vietnam hands all, had simply had enough war; the cameraman was on the verge of a nervous breakdown and two days later quit and returned to Hong Kong. The correspondent decided that rather than go up and cover the morning's attack, he would get his story where he was. He first interviewed the young company commander of the unit in reserve, and then he asked if the officer would have a squad of his men move down the street (taken two days before) and go through the motion of clearing a house, just as if this were the attack taking place, or about to take place, three blocks away. The officer, who seemed delighted to be on television, agreed, and a squad was duly placed at the disposal of the television crew. Now playing Hollywood Marines in their brief time-out from a very real and deadly war, the squad moved about a block down the street to a vacant, half-gutted house while the television camera churned. There, for the sake of pictorial realism, they were asked to throw a smoke grenade into the house. One of them did, and a plume of white smoke boiled from the interior and rose into the air. Before they had a chance to walk back up the block, North Vietnamese mortar rounds, apparently aimed at the smoke plume, rained on the area, killing two Marines in the headquarters compound and killing and wounding several South Vietnamese soldiers in the immediate vicinity. Neither the television crew nor their Marine "extras" suffered anything more than fright.

There have been a few staging incidents in which stories were fabricated out of whole cloth. But staging is usually an attempt to approximate a genuine story that, for one reason or another, cannot actually be filmed. It is a vice common to every form of journalism, including newspaper and magazine photography, but the vice seems more strongly motivated in television and is certainly much more dangerous, because of the medium's power and because it purports to show reality, not just describe it. The practice is not unknown in the print media, either, though it is probably rarer and certainly harder to detect. In May of 1966, during the fighting between Government forces and Buddhist rebels in Danang, a group of reporters was caught in a crossfire after having trooped to a Buddhist pagoda, the last center of rebel resistance, to attend what they thought would be a press conference. Three of them were hit by grenade fragments after leaving the pagoda on their way back to the U.S. Marine–operated press center in the city. One Reuters correspondent arrived at the press center shaken and scared but already composing in his head the lead for his version of the most dramatic story of the week—only to find that his colleague, who had never left the press-center bar, had already filed a hair-raising "I was there" account of the incident. With the exposure of such practices, it is little wonder that public confidence in the integrity of the news they receive has suffered some damage and that the press has acquired its own credibility gap.

A much more common practice does not really stage the *story* at all but simply applies cosmetics to improve its looks. Although seemingly a lesser vice, "cosmetizing" has implications even more serious than those of staging in order to make up for a lost story. In both cases the television reporter has become a movie director; but in the former instance the motivation of the reporter or producer is the desire to change reality, however slightly, for reasons of personal aesthetics, sense of drama, or simply the convenience of his cameramen. The logical projected extreme of such a fusion of the reporter's and the director's roles leads to visions that outdo Orwell. And the very tight triangulation of commerce–show-biz–journalism in the production and broadcasting of television news and public-affairs programming makes the danger quite serious. During the Arab-Israeli war in June, 1967, an American network-television crew, arriving on the Sinai front after the fighting, asked a group of Israeli soldiers to put on Arab kaffiyahs and play dead around the burnt-out hulk of an Egyptian tank. Two other Israelis were given the roles of prisoner and captor, coming over a dune and into the field of the television camera on cue. After the crew had their story on film, the dead "Arabs" rose and went about their business, like a bunch of latter-day Lazaruses. It was a standard war scene and must have occurred in reality any number of times in the course of the war—after all, a lot of Arabs *were* killed, a lot of tanks *were* burnt, and a lot of prisoners taken. But then the same thing can be said of scenes from fictional TV series, and "Combat," "Rat Patrol," and "Garrison's Guerrillas" are *not* journalism. Further, it is but a short step from re-creating what clearly did happen to creating what one *thinks* happened, and then to the fabrication of what one thinks *should* have happened. Nor do the scenes themselves have to be "staged." A picture story can be made to mean many different things by the narration added to it.

An example of what can happen in this respect was offered in the summer of 1969 by a protest sent to the F.C.C. by a former news writer for WPIX-TV in New York, a station owned by the *Daily News*. According to the complainant, the statement was subscribed to by three other former WPIX writers. The charge made was distortion of news film by the station. Particular allegations were (1) that the station ran Vietnam film as much as four days old as a "today" story, (2) that during the Soviet occupation of Czechoslovakia WPIX used a crowd scene filmed in Bucharest, Rumania, and superimposed on the picture the legends "Prague" and "Via Satellite" and also that the narrator of the piece was a stringer in Vienna pretending he was on a Prague street corner, and (3) that film for a story on demonstrations at San Francisco State College was taken the day before the incident it purported to illustrate. Whether or not these specific allegations are true in whole or in part with re-spect to WPIX, they are not altogether unheard-of practices in the television news business. They are corruptions born out of the current fusion of news and show-biz concepts and values under the intense pressure of commercial competition for the attention of the greatest number of viewers and according to the tastes and values of the lowest common denominator.

The same values are visible in a less dramatic but perhaps even more important area: *selection* of news stories. Again, Vietnam is a prime example. Television reporters in Vietnam are acutely aware that what their New York offices want, above all, are action stories, known in the trade as bang-bang. They are not as a rule told this in so many words. They simply know from experience what is most likely to be used on the evening news program—and for a reporter whose professional reputation (and a portion of his income) is made by what is *used,* not what is put in the can, words are un-necessary. On this score Mike Wallace said that during the time he was in Vietnam, "some of the correspondents kept a kind of score-card as to which pieces were and were not used and why, and it did seem as though an inordinate number of combat pieces were used compared with some first-rate pieces in the political area or the pacification area or nonbloody stories."*

Vietnam has long been a big story, often *the* big story, for Amer-ican reporters. On television, however, it has often seemed that Vietnam's importance as a *news* event is outweighed by its impor-tance as a dramatic event. How else explain the displacement of perhaps significant news and analysis—a political story, for in-stance, that might presage a change in the situation—by the cover-age of search-and-destroy operation Number 3,468, which is indis-tinguishable, both in terms of pictorial and audio features and in terms of the operation's achievements or significance, from opera-tion Number 346 or, for that matter, from operation Number 34? The public is thus "getting what it wants" in the news in very much the same manner it gets what it wants with "Peyton Place" and "Twelve O'Clock High." It is little wonder, then, that a people which gets two-thirds of its news from television acquired a superfi-

* "The Whole World Is Watching," P.B.L.

cial, unreal view of the Vietnam situation as the same black and
white, good guys and bad guys conflict that the Johnson Administration tried to promote. Although this was not the view held by
many television correspondents working in Vietnam, most of whom
have been men of moderate to considerable professional talent and
integrity, it took the 1968 Tet offensive to disabuse television—its
principal commentators and its audience—of this view.

Contamination: Propaganda and the News

The inability to draw a strong, sharp line between journalism
and show business—which is ultimately to say, between fact and
fiction—is one of the most critical problems in modern-day American journalism because of the crucial role television occupies in
conveying news. The case should not, of course, be overstated, and
it is the opposite of my intention to foster paranoia toward the
press; my purpose is, rather, to point out what are serious dangers
to the press. The quality of television news, both in terms of the
caliber of its people and the professionalism of its standards, has
improved considerably over the years. But that improvement falls
somewhat short of revolution. Probably the most hopeful aspect of
the picture is that many television newsmen—reporters, producers,
and news executives alike—have become increasingly aware of and
vigilant toward these problems and vices and the special responsibilities they bear.

One of the difficulties after drawing the line between fact and
fiction is in making the viewer aware of it, and this is a part of the
problem over which the newsman and the television news departments have absolutely no control. The problem arises because
fiction—outright, announced fiction—can look very much like fact
and often purports to be or to represent fact. What we find in the
"entertainment," or avowedly show-biz, side of the equation is a
reversal of the fact-fiction relationship. Theoretically, television has
two functions vis-à-vis the viewing public: to inform them and to
entertain them, with great predominance given the latter. Theoretically, the two functions are separate, but as we have seen, in reality

the values and practices of show-business impinge upon and corrupt the process of informing. In like manner the desire to inform invades the area of entertainment, and a host of regular network television programs, particularly dramatic series, have become fiction-*cum*-propaganda, consciously or inadvertently developing and nourishing attitudes among viewers which affect their reception of information provided by journalists—sometimes creating a built-in hostility to that information, but in any case tending to wash out whatever line might exist between fact and fiction on television. This process is accelerated by the imperative of realism and "authenticity" in dramatic presentations, even of the most banal sort (actually, the more banal the program, the more important those values become).

Take, as the most prominent and flagrant example of this phenomenon, the great gaggle of television dramatic series devoted to the trials and tribulations of policemen. A few that spring immediately to mind are "N.Y.P.D.," "Adam-12," "Dragnet," "Ironside," and "The F.B.I." All of them are technically well done fictional propaganda vehicles for specific police departments (New York City, Los Angeles, San Francisco, and of course, the Federal Bureau of Investigation) as well as for law-enforcement groups and attitudes in general. Possessing the ideal ingredients of danger, action, and simple but effective ready-made plots, the genre has always been a sure-fire winner, but it seems exceptionally successful today with so much public concern over crime in the streets, student uprisings, civil-rights and antiwar demonstrations, and the general issue of law and order. Now, the line between serious fictional drama and reality has always been provisional at best. As art, the former is involved with "truth" as much as, and to a depth inaccessible to, fact-bound journalism; in the same manner comedy and satire have always been intimately involved in the subject matter of journalism. They are individual and independent visions of truth and the meaning of reality, to be judged as such, free of any other considerations or responsibilities. The dramatic series named above, however, are about as independent as the editorial board of *Pravda*. Not only are such shows dependent on the political and social views and attitudes of network executives and advertisers, but, more importantly, they are dependent on the views and public-relations interests of the organizations they portray. The case of one such program reveals a general pattern.

David Susskind's production company developed and produced "N.Y.P.D." The subject matter, policemen and their work, was already a proven success, as was the gimmick of using "actual case histories" for the story basis (both established by the original "Dragnet" series of prehistoric times; "Dragnet" also established, with its twelve-word vocabulary and its pseudodocumentary style, the effectiveness of the illusion of "authenticity"). "N.Y.P.D.," however, was going to add a couple of wrinkles. It would (and did) incorporate a black cop in its cast of detectives. And it would be rigorously authentic, to the finest details, in its portrayal of police work in New York City, i.e., it would be a model of technical realism. For this purpose the producers required the full cooperation of the *real* N.Y.P.D., the New York Police Department, and that cooperation was forthcoming—but with strings. Before it would agree to the scheme, the real-life N.Y.P.D. demanded the right to cancel shows it disapproved of, not simply at the time they were completed and put in the can but up until two weeks prior to their scheduled broadcast—presumably in case somebody changed his mind, or in case Jacques Nevard, N.Y.P.D.'s minister of information, was late in screening the episodes.

For some viewers such a story may come as a surprise. For others it simply documents a situation that has long been palpably obvious, and for them it is self-evident that similar procedures are to some degree in force in the case of other series that rely on the cooperation of the organization they portray. No one who watches "The F.B.I.," however occasionally, could imagine a truly critical look at the bureau and its operations in one of the show's episodes. One cannot conceive of "Dragnet" or "Adam-12" approaching the question of policemen and their work from any but an inside, public-relations viewpoint. This kind of abject prostitution is not entirely the invention of television. It has long been a standard procedure in the movie industry, where whores are made when they are not born. This is particularly true in war movies requiring (as most all of them do) the cooperation of the Army, Navy, Marine Corps, or Air Force. *Dr. Strangelove* not only could get no cooperation from the military, but it was lucky not to have been made the object of a pacification program. *The Green Berets,* on the other hand, got so much cooperation that one would not have been surprised to learn that the Vietnam war had been set back six months on its account. The movies, however, do not double as the nation's principal source of news and information; and the frequency, availability, and consequently the power of television create a much more serious conditioning problem than the storied corruption of the movie industry ever could.

This is not just a convenient example. The police problem is one of the most serious, complex, and perilous issues facing contemporary American society. A report published in June, 1969, by the National Commission on the Causes and Prevention of Violence found that across the nation the police were becoming politicized and polarized to an extent that endangers the structure of democracy. The report, prepared under the direction of Jerome H. Skolnick, of the Center of the Study of Law and Society at the University of California at Berkeley, documented the growing political power of police organizations (a power far out of proportion to their numbers), the effectiveness of such organizations in pressuring political institutions, their tendency to equate dissent with subversion, and a growing public acceptance of both the attitudes and the extracurricular political activities of these public servants in blue. It is not cop-baiting to observe that, for reasons often beyond the control of the overburdened and underpaid policeman, the attitudes and activities of the police and their effect on the rest of society pose not just serious but critical problems for democracy in our time. But how are the millions who regularly view these television dramatizations and are emotionally and intellectually affected by them to view an objective study of, say, the basic disputes between the police and ghetto dwellers? They have seen, time and again, every variety of police critic—demonstrator, reporter, reformist politician—not only portrayed in consistently unflattering and unsavory roles but also, with equal consistency, linked to the causes of rising crime rates, disrespect for authority, and the general dissolution of American society. The Neanderthal social theories of J. Edgar Hoover, Sam Yorty, and the average chief of police come alive several times a week on the home screen as dramatizations of "true case histories from the files of. . . ." In this respect one cannot divorce television news from the quality and integrity of television entertainment. It is little wonder that a medium which spends so much of its time and energy developing such an audience and which has acquired such a financial stake in the goodwill and cooperation of law-enforcement propagandists is less than reckless in presenting news and public-affairs programs that challenge either.

The problem does not confine itself to the attitude of the average television viewer toward only the police and their critics. Television news executives can talk about the independence of their operations all they like (and they like to a great deal), but those operations can never be very independent of the attitudes and values developed in the average viewer by the medium's overall product, whether the issue be crime in the streets, the Vietnam war, or Presidential politics. This is one area the television networks might consider when, and if, they contemplate the apparent contradiction between their immense power to influence public opinion (which is a fact, in spite of its use by Spiro T. Agnew) and the widespread public support for Agnew's attack on their news presentation.

Independence is also compromised by sponsor attitudes, such as those cited by a representative of Westinghouse Electric (which has its own network) during the darker days of blacklisting:

> We buy "Studio One" as a package from CBS through our agency, McCann Erickson. These two businesses, as well as all of us at Westinghouse, have a great stake in our capitalistic society. It is therefore in our own best interests never to engage in any activities that would jeopardize the free-enterprise system.*

And Harry J. Skornia in *Television and the News* quotes a president of Columbia Artists Management as laying down the following rule for performers:

> The public performer . . . must observe an axiom of show business, which is not to engage in contentious nonconformism.

* John Cogley, *Report on Blacklisting*, Vol. II: *Radio-Television* (New York: Fund for the Republic, 1956), p. 30.

. . . Active participation in politics . . . is incompatible with his profession. . . . Judgment of a performer's behavior is on a public-relations level. Wherein merit may lie on any question is irrelevant.

Considerable changes have taken place in the industry since those gems of wisdom were uttered, but hardly a revolution. Going back to the contrasting treatment of the Smothers brothers and Bob Hope, the former presumably "jeopardized" the system, whereas the latter did not. In the context of the second quote, Hope's plugging of the Johnson Vietnam policy was obviously an engagement in conformism, whereas the brothers Smothers had been guilty of "contentious nonconformism." The fact that much of any network's revenue comes from people holding such attitudes creates a perilous atmosphere for the operation of an independent, "call the chips where they fall" news department.

The intrusion of show-biz values into informational programming, the need to include elements of conflict whether they exist naturally in the subject matter or not, the compulsion to emphasize the dramatic and focus on the bizarre at the expense of distorting reality, and the attempt to fabricate drama where it is not sufficiently present dangerously compromise the integrity and credibility of television news and must inevitably deepen public mistrust and hostility toward the press, even as they succeed in attracting viewers and raising ratings. These corruptions are matched by the ideological conditioning of audiences by entertainment programming. Taken together, they constitute a major reason why, as Robert MacNeil states, "relatively few documentaries really delve into the acute problems of our time," and why the electronic press today, while under attack from several directions, lacks the moral courage necessary for an adequate defense.

Intrusion: Affecting the News While Reporting It

One of the most frequent criticisms of television news in recent years has been aimed at its intrusion into events and its tendency to seriously affect and even change those events. The most dramatic examples of this intrusion have taken place in the streets of America's cities during demonstrations, riots, and other crowd situations. But television, it has been widely noted, intrudes into more sedentary events as well, as a visit to one of the national political conventions will show. Television, as a matter of fact, has almost revolutionized the form, if not the substance, of those events. There are two aspects to this intrusion. The first is the effect of television's physical presence: the cameras, lights, recording equipment, remote vans, cables, and the men who operate all these. Even a single crew—a correspondent, a cameraman, and a sound man—accounts for an impressive array of equipment, and it is technologically very difficult for television news to cover a story unobtrusively, as a newspaper reporter can. The second aspect of intrusion is the effect that coverage has on a continuing event. Criticism of TV news and its effect on riot situations has involved both these aspects. For instance, many critics have pointed to the undeniable fact that people tend to act differently with the arrival of a television crew at the scene of a demonstration and that the situation often becomes more volatile then. It has also been charged that in numerous cases people have converged on the scenes of riots after having seen on television what and where the action was.

Two points should be made here that are usually ignored. The first is that both forms of intrusion, the intrusion of physical presence and the intrusion of reporting an event while it is still happening, are matters that involve *all* the press, not just television (though television's effect is much more dramatic and powerful). A group of reporters suddenly arriving on the scene of a disturbance, demonstration, meeting, or whatever, even without TV lights and cameras, can be quite noticeable and affecting. Newspaper reporting can alter a "live" event as well, though not as instantly, as television. The second point is that reporting has affected and altered events and situations since the beginning of journalism. This is a truism that, unfortunately, is too often lost sight of in attacks on the press. No event, no situation, no story, can ever quite be the same after it has been reported, no matter how dispassionately and objectively it may have been done. Sometimes the result is salutary, sometimes unfortunate, but the general phenomenon is unavoidable—and unavoidably the price as well as the dividend of a free press.

In the case of WBAI and the anti-Semitism furor, a manageable controversy that had already begun to recede was lit anew and altered almost beyond recognition by a story appearing in *The New York Times* three weeks after the incident in question. It altered the immediate situation, a fairly rational controversy between the station and some of its listeners, and like live coverage of a riot by television, it drew people to the scene who would never have been there otherwise. It stimulated organizations whose directors knew nothing of the total context of the station's programming to denounce WBAI as anti-Semitic, "a party to the crime of genocide," and to call for its extinction by the F.C.C. The *Times*'s story was straight and objective, as were its subsequent stories on the issue. The effect, however, was a gross distortion of the situation. Should the *Times,* then, not have run the story? Not even WBAI's management would have suggested that. What happened was unfortunate, not only for WBAI but also for the political and racial climate in the city at the time. But had the *Times* not printed the story of the U.F.T.'s complaint to the F.C.C., it would have demonstrated professional irresponsibility: the suppression of relevant news. It was not *The New York Times* that was the first cause of the uproar but a polarized and increasingly hysterical political and racial atmosphere. Indeed, there is some reason to believe now that the controversy and the subsequent dialogues and discussions, public and private, which the story provoked may even have had a healthy effect in the long run.

Skornia feels, as do many others, that broadcasting needs to establish controls "to insure against its being a news-*maker.*" He cites the case of a Chicago radio station that was charged by a Coles County, Illinois, sheriff with being responsible for student demonstrations in Charleston, Illinois, after having reported rumors that a water fight was to take place at a certain time in a certain place. "The airing of such rumors," he wrote, "without checking, attracted hundreds of outsiders to the expected trouble area and at the same time caused many students to try to make the predicted 'show' a reality." He also cites a case in which the practice of staging created a news event:

> Early in 1960, Governor Buford Ellington of Tennessee accused the CBS television crew sent to Nashville of instigating a racial demonstration. Apparently the cameramen, and those to whom they were accountable, wearied of having nothing to report. The crew and trip were costing CBS money. To liven things up, a few local citizens were enlisted as actors. Before long, the situation was no longer peaceful or quiet. Television had *created* news, so it could report on it.

Such practices are not only professionally unethical; they are also socially dangerous in the extreme. What Skornia fails to point out, however, is that legitimate reporting of legitimate news can have the same effect on subsequent developments. Many people genuinely believe that the press, and particularly television, should not report bad news. Ridiculous as that sounds, it is a conclusion many editors and broadcasters have arrived at, particularly in the aftermath of Chicago. At the 1969 convention of the American Newspaper Publishers Association, Stewart Macdonald, manager of the ANPA Newspaper Information Service, told the publishers:

> The evidence today is that many people do not understand the press, do not see why the press has to cover bad and unpleasant news, do not see why the press must report the violence of our troubled times, do not want to look at the record of misdoing and corruption that dots the pages of the daily newspaper.

Against the truly appalling excesses he cites, Skornia suggests that if television cannot discipline its own house, then "far more rigid controls" by public agencies are called for. Unfortunately, such controls are far more likely to be exercised on the basis of the supposed damage done than on the basis of unethical press behavior.

To quote again from *Television and the News:*

> Control over the *description* of events in effect gives television a large measure of control over what appears to have happened.

By what it fails to show, television prevents an *occurrence,* however real, from becoming *news.* By what it promotes, or shows, it *creates* both news and history. What TV shows becomes news, however un-news-*worthy* it might be by more reflective standards.

Although there is a great deal of truth in each of these statements, what is left out is that all of the above is also true of the print media and that television differs only with respect to its greater impact and the extra vices caused by the dynamics of show-business values in the news. Both of the above statements can be applied to the more powerful of America's newspapers, such as *The New York Times,* which often sets the pace and arbitrates what is and is not news for television. One of the major criticisms leveled at TV news, and one many television newsmen make themselves, is that it is too dependent on *The New York Times* and the Associated Press for its coverage and story selection both of local and of national and international news as well. What Skornia is criticizing are real problems, but they are problems that television only amplifies; their source lies in the fact that, unfortunately, subomniscient and less than God-like creatures report the news. What the advent of television has done is to make the impact of the press more powerful, for good or for ill, than ever before. It is this fact that has begun to frighten people (aside from particular corruptions and transgressions in the profession), politician and citizen alike.

Part of the problem is that we are presented today with the means of far greater and more immediate communication than was ever before possible and that, on the one hand, powerful interests have largely subjected those means to the task of selling cars and deodorants and, on the other hand, many (and not a few in positions of considerable power) object, as Walter Cronkite pointed out, to the very communication itself. It is perhaps for this reason that television's (and journalism's) effect on events, on history, is almost invariably discussed as an assumed evil and the instances cited almost always negative. But what of the television documentary or newspaper series that uncovers and points a national finger at a major problem, such as hunger in America or the safety conditions in coal mines, and thereby initiates government action? What about the role of television in bringing the civil-rights movement of the early 1960's into the national consciousness? For many city officials, mine-owners, and southerners these were reprehensible acts of a medium out to cause trouble for private gain. I am not trying to argue that the considerable vices and corruptions in the press, and especially in the electronic press, be ignored or discounted—far from it. I *am* trying to suggest that we should not identify the genuine vices of modern-day journalism with the effect of its basic role in a free society. That the press and its activities affect and alter events and history itself is unarguable. That is its purpose, after all, and when it does not, who needs it? The fact that vast numbers of Americans do not understand this truism in today's period of high literacy and wide access is genuinely frightening. It is much more frightening than the ready use that demagogues and bureaucrats are willing to make of it.

One of the most moving and dramatic examples of the effect of the press (in this case, television) on events and public reaction was that offered in the BBC's contribution to the Public Broadcast Lab's "The Whole World Is Watching." A BBC reporter and crew covering the Nigeria-Biafra fighting were on hand, cameras and tape recorder running, when Nigerian troops captured a Biafran prisoner. The correspondent asked the officer-in-charge if the Nigerians were going to shoot the prisoner. The officer responded that he would be taken to their headquarters. The prisoner said a few words in English into the BBC mike and was then led off *and shot,* on camera. At this point P.B.L. correspondent Revel Guest commented: "The sight of this murder on their screens in their own homes so shattered public opinion [in Britain] that there was an outcry and the Nigerians were forced to respond." The following sequence showed the same BBC correspondent and crew, and the same Nigerian officer. But this time the officer was not shooting any prisoners. He was about to be shot himself; and he was shot, executed on camera, in response to that outcry. Guest continued:

> It was television that made them execute their grim justice on this man. The question as to whether this should have been

shown in full is still being debated. Television executives, faced with the problem of whether to show scenes of this kind, had to take into account the effect of world opinion on complicated local issues.

Now, there is nothing very complicated at all in a group of soldiers killing a newly captured prisoner; on the contrary, it is one of those very *un*-complicated, primitive brutalities common to every group and every nation, no matter what their pretensions to civilization might be. The effect of the reaction of world opinion toward such a brutality on the complex issues of the Nigeria-Biafra dispute should perhaps be a concern for television and other press executives but only insofar as the news operations for which those executives are responsible seriously attempt to elucidate those issues and place them in perspective. Surely such concern should not lead to the suppression of stories such as the above or attempts to mitigate the impact with basically irrelevant material, like showing a model prison camp afterward. The one is censorship; the other, propaganda. We have seen the same question posed many times in this country with respect to reporting of the Vietnam war. That, too, in many respects, is a very complicated local issue (although it has been a long time since it was *simply* a local issue). Reporters and their superiors have repeatedly been implored and harangued by "responsible" officials to keep the nasty stuff in perspective—or not to use it at all. From the battle of Ap Bac to the siege of Khe Sanh and after, the press has been cautioned about obscuring the "big picture" with independent and contrary details, and the negative effects of their work on the public back home has been constantly thrown in their faces. To the extent that the American press corps in Vietnam has rejected the responsibilities assigned to them by earnest officials, it has done the nation a singular service in providing Americans with the only realistic view of the war available to them. To the extent that the Vietnam press corps, or some of it, has accepted such responsibilities, it has become little more than an echo of official foolishness.

This is not to dismiss the primary importance of the "big picture." Indeed, the most signal failure of the contemporary press may well be the failure to provide its consumers with knowledge of sufficient depth and perspective, the failure to relate isolated facts adequately to a larger reality. What is frequently offered the press, however, and particularly in Vietnam, is a "big picture" of highly selective composition, a distortion handed down from above, shaped to fit the contours of policy. Nor is this to dismiss the question of the social responsibility of the press for the effects of its operations. This question will remain the most profound and difficult issue the profession faces, and it will be debated as long as a free press persists. To what extent can, or *should,* a journalist concern himself with anything but the truth? There really is no answer, except in the most specific of instances, and not always then. For instance: A reporter covering big-city crime learns the name of a key witness in a gangland killing. If he uses the name when he files his story, he is jeopardizing the life of the witness, the case of the prosecution, and the interests of the community (the apprehension of the murderers) for a detail unimportant to his readers. The proper course for the reporter to follow would seem fairly clear. But only in such simple cases is the answer to the question so easy. In other instances the same concerns—an individual's welfare, the secrets of an official body, and a journalist's presumption as to the interests of the community and how they are best served—can be poison to the very concept of a free press and the democratic society it serves. (Cf. the Bay of Pigs.)

When riots began to flare in the ghettos of America's major cities, considerable attention began to be focused on the activities of the press and the effects of press coverage and reporting, especially radio and television. A great deal was heard about the exacerbation of unstable situations by the presence of TV camera crews and by live radio and television coverage. There was much talk about the need for "restraint" and self-regulation by the news media, and news organizations in a number of cities adopted voluntary "codes" for handling news of civil disturbances. Such codes, highly recommended by the *Report of the National Advisory Commission on Civil Disorders* (the Kerner Report), generally provide for a delay in the reporting of riots or incipient riots of from fifteen minutes to an indefinite period of time. The reason for this is the assertion, accepted by many newsmen and news executives themselves, that live reporting over the air or even immediately after the fact tends to attract curious citizens and reenforcements for the rioters, both of whom get in the way of the police and endanger their own persons—in other words, it tends to enflame the situation all the more. There is no question but that this does indeed happen. But another aspect of the problem, which was largely ignored in the crisis atmosphere of the time, was pointed out in the Fall, 1968, issue of the *Columbia Journalism Review*. In an article entitled "The Perils of Self-Management" Richard M. Harnett, a U.P.I. reporter in San Francisco, wrote:

> When local radio and television stations [in San Francisco] declined to broadcast the news that police riot units had sealed off streets and raced through the area shooting out the streetlights to hamper snipers, they abdicated a responsibility to their listeners. Lack of knowledge about what was going on in that part of the city might have resulted in unnecessary danger to innocent persons living there or elsewhere.

Here, it seems to me, we are at the very heart of the question, however we answer it. Whether you wish to call such practices press restraint, self-regulation, self-management, or suppression, the fact is that a very basic, profound decision not to report the news has been made, whether those who made the decision realize it or not. The essential function of the press in a free society is to provide information to a free citizenry who are presumed competent to evaluate that information and make up their minds as to their best course of action or inaction, as the case may be. The very structure and fabric of democracy is founded upon this presumption. The inescapable implication of the "codes" is precisely the opposite: The populace is *not* competent; it must be protected from certain kinds of information at certain times. Perhaps this is true. But if we decide that it is, let us be honest enough to admit that the principles underlying the democratic form of government are anachronisms and should be done away with before they lead us to perdition.

To simplify (perhaps to oversimplify), the first and fundamental duty of the press is to inform the tired and hungry commuter that if he follows his customary route home from work today, he may well be shot, stoned, fire-bombed, tear-gassed, or busted by a nightstick. Its responsibility for assisting the police in the maintenance of law and order, however important it may be deemed, is surely secondary. Many will argue that the truth lies somewhere between these extremes, that the responsibility of the press in informing the citizen and its responsibility toward law and order are one and the same and can therefore be easily reconciled or at least balanced. This may be the most dangerous aspect of the entire situation—dangerous in part because of its subtlety—more dangerous than burning ghettos, looted stores, rampaging mobs, and cops out of their senses. It is a frame of mind which lacks the awareness, necessary to the maintenance of any democracy, that *balance* is an abstraction, that democracy by its very nature can never be a well-oiled and thoroughly efficient machine, that freedom has its price, and that the price of freedom like the cost of living can rise to seemingly unbearable heights. The idea, so prevalent today, that the substance and forms of democracy can be traded piecemeal for civil safety and social convenience constitutes a far greater danger to that social structure than riots, insurrections, revolution, or Chinese hordes. And the almost hungry willingness of many average Americans to concede such erosions, on the assumption that they are provisional, temporary, extraordinary, and directed at those crazy black bastards across town anyway, makes this reporter fear for the future of American democracy. I could not assent too emphatically with another point made by Harnett in the same article:

> News media have battled long and hard to keep anyone else from playing God over the information people should be given on current issues. It would be ironic if well-intentioned news executives themselves moved into the throne as arbiters of what is good for the people to know and not to know. Certainly news executives should . . . [give] their staffs greater guidance on handling racial news. But such guidance must be fully explainable in the context of the proved bedrock of American journalism—the premise that the press itself does not decide what is good or bad for society but informs the people so they can decide.

A fifteen- to thirty-minute delay in the reporting of riot news may not seem unreasonable (except to a motorist driving into the troubled area during that period or to a resident of the area who has left her children in the care of a teen-age babysitter to shop downtown). It generally takes a newsman at least that long to find out just what is going on anyway. But many city officials and some news executives have urged far longer periods of "blackout" as well as selective censorship and news-management on the part of news organizations. It should be noted that the suppression of riot news in San Francisco mentioned by Harnett was agreed to by the San Francisco *Chronicle* and its television station, KRON-TV, the latter presently under investigation by the F.C.C. for managing news in the corporate interests of the former, not for managing news in the interests of civil peace. The Kerner Report, although recommending the adoption of limited "codes"—that is to say, voluntary agreements among news organizations in local areas to delay for limited periods the reporting of riot outbreaks—had this to say about any further restrictions on press coverage—voluntary or otherwise:

> It would be imprudent and even dangerous to downplay coverage in the hope that censored reporting of inflammatory incidents somehow will diminish violence. . . . To attempt to ignore these events or portray them as something other than what they are can only diminish confidence in the media and increase the effectiveness of those who monger rumors and the fears of those who listen.

In addition, the commission discovered that both official and private criticisms of the press and charges as to the effect of press coverage on these incidents reflected a basic misunderstanding of the entire situation. The most telling criticisms leveled at the press by the Kerner Report were quite the opposite of those made by most officials and private critics. It found, for instance, that

> many of the inaccuracies of fact, tone and mood were due to the failure of reporters and editors to ask tough enough questions about official reports. . . . The initial estimates [of the amount

of monetary damage in Detroit caused by riots] were not the independent judgment of reporters or editors. They came from
beleaguered government officials. But the news media gave currency to these errors. Reporters uncritically accepted, and editors uncritically published, the inflated figures.

Far from feeding the fires of rebellion and riot by focusing on the
rioters and exhibiting bias in favor of them, the press tended to
contribute to the chaos in a far more fundamental way: by its
failure to report fairly and accurately, or in any depth, the problems and grievances of the black and the poor—by presenting itself
to the ghetto resident as just another section of the wall between the
black ghetto and the white man's world. The commission made the
following finding:

> The media report and write from the standpoint of a white
> man's world. . . . [The] press . . . repeatedly, if uncon-
> sciously, reflects the biases, the paternalism, the indifference of
> white America. . . . Editors and reporters . . . acknowl-
> edged that the police and city officials are their main—and
> sometimes their only—source of information. It was also noted
> that most reporters who cover civil disturbances tend to arrive
> with the police and stay close to them—often for safety, and
> often because they learn where the action is at the same time
> as the authorities—and thus buttress the ghetto impression that
> police and press work together and toward the same ends (an
> impression that may come as a surprise to many within the
> ranks of police and press).

With respect to television coverage of civil disorders and the
many and loud demands made for "balance" and "restraint" in TV
reporting, the commission suggested that

> television sometimes may have leaned over too far backward
> in seeking balance and restraint. By stressing interviews, many
> with whites in predominantly Negro neighborhoods, and by em-
> phasizing control scenes rather than riotous action, television
> news broadcasting may have given a distorted picture of what
> the disorders were all about.

The most controversial, and courageous, finding of the entire Kerner Report (and one that shocked and angered Lyndon Johnson) was an admission of what should have been perfectly obvious. One of the causes of civil disorder and violence in the streets was the fact that, contrary to all the hallowed Sunday-school homilies and political banalities, it *paid!* Official ears, usually deaf to quiet reasoning, verbal complaints and grievances, and properly channeled charges of injustices and deprivation, were suddenly opened by the sounds of breaking glass, screaming sirens, and gun shots. This was true from police-department reaction to charges of police mistreatment to Washington's sudden interest in the problems of the cities and the urban ghettos. This was heresy coming from a commission appointed and charged by the President (who commanded its deletion), but it was the gut truth of the situation—a truth the press should have been digging into and reporting long before the report was published. It did not. The commission reported its opinion that the press has not "communicated to the majority of their audience—which is white—a sense of the degradation, misery and hopelessness of life in the ghetto." This has been a far greater failing and poses a far greater danger to the community and the nation than the risks involved in the full, unexpurgated reporting of our explosive racial scene. It is a sad day for American journalism when a Presidential commission proves to be a less timid, more radically thorough reporter of a domestic problem than the nation's press.

Far from being too irresponsible, much of the nation's press is often too responsible—responsible for values and concerns which lie outside the scope of their profession and are often in direct contradiction to its imperatives. A professional conservatism and timidity fostered by the dominating influence of business and show business in the news media and by a strong identification with the problems and outlook of the political and economic Establishment on the part of media executives have worn away the substance of the free press from the inside far more to date than any assaults or threats of assault from without the profession. The duty of every professional to the public is first and foremost his own particular function. A doctor has many responsibilities as a citizen—up to, and only up to, the point where they interfere with the care of his patient, even if that patient is a mass murderer. The structuring of the priorities of a journalist's responsibilities can be no less rigorous in protecting the right of the people to know and the integrity of the means for that knowledge—even when he or society must pay a painful price for it.

New Directions: The Pseudoevent and Access to the Media

One of the besetting problems of modern-day journalism, particularly electronic journalism, is its vulnerability to manipulation and exploitation by other groups and forces. The technique par excellence developed for this purpose is the "pseudoevent," a fabricated happening usually planned with one purpose in mind: that it will be reported. In fact, the reporting is a calculated *part* of the event; it is its culmination. The employment of this technique requires two things: (1) on the part of the manipulator, some power and influence or a considerable knowledge of the psychology and operational machinery of the media (or both) and (2) on the part of the media, a certain lack of judgment and will, sometimes helped by a masochistic predisposition to be used.

This technique is a key to understanding the relationship between the press and the executive branch of government in this country and the ability of any Administration to exploit the press and the credulity of the people almost at will. In 1966, when scheduled hearings by the Senate Foreign Relations Committee under Senator J. William Fulbright threatened to stir up increasing opposition to the Administration's Vietnam policy, Lyndon Baines Johnson set up one of the classic pseudoevents in recent history— and one of the most successful. He pulled out of his hat another Honolulu conference, a summit meeting of those running the Vietnam war on the allied side. It looked at the outset like a set-up job whose sole and single purpose was to take the news spotlight away from the Fulbright hearings. When all the results were in, when the accomplishments of the conference were reported, that supposition became historical fact in the minds of most observers.

The ruse, transparent as it was from the beginning, was successful—particularly with the television networks.

These organizations, while they debate among themselves as to the importance to the nation of such events as the Fulbright hearings on Vietnam (CBS chose reruns of "I Love Lucy" because they make more money), feel constrained to cover, at considerable expense, the comings, goings, and utterances of the President to a degree that is little short of slavish. If the President wishes to hold a press conference, no matter how short the notice or how banal and unimportant his prepared utterances, the networks not only carry it, but they carry it live. There is little reason (and no evidence) to doubt that the President of the United States could get live, prime-time coverage on all three networks, if he requested it, to wish his wife happy birthday. A number of television's critics have pointed to the tendency of the medium to elevate the banal and lower the profound so that both exist side by side. When it comes to the President of the United States, the banal and the profound sometimes trade places.

A similar, though more complicated, situation applies to the print media. The utterances of the President are invariably front-page news, even if they are simply observations on the weather. The opinions and assertions of other officials often receive press treatment more in accordance with their position in the Administration hierarchy than with the genuine significance of their actions or statements.

This ability of the President and his Administration to draw the focus of the media, almost at will, becomes particularly noticeable at the time of political campaigning. This is the time when the President's press secretary generally keeps himself short of wind by repeating, "Gentlemen, this is a nonpolitical address." Political campaigns are the springtime of the pseudoevent, and various forms and versions of the phenomenon seem at such times to comprise a good 50 per cent of the news. Senators and Congressmen about to run for reelection don't go home to campaign, they go on "fact-finding" tours in connection with a current or projected "investigation." Dams that have been holding back the same amount of water for decades and are unlikely to alter their performance in future years suddenly receive a Congressional or Senatorial visit, which requires a "nonpolitical" speech, which obtains a spot on the evening news, at least locally. Congressman Blah, for the first time in the entire controversy, suddenly has something to say on the subject of the Vietnam war. It amounts to three innocuous sentences out of a speech comprising three hundred sentences, but it earns him a spot on network evening news programs and gets his name and picture in the papers the next day. Another Congressman decides it is his patriotic duty to travel to Vietnam and get the facts from the horse's mouth. He spends five days in Saigon, alternating his time between air-conditioned briefings and air-conditioned cocktail parties, and returns, all at government expense, to impress his constituents with the dangers he risked for their sakes and with his new omniscience concerning the most important problem facing the nation. And how does the press conduct itself? For the most part it falls right into line, as though it were required by law to treat such craven abuse of the public's credulity as a serious news story. It is an abject surrender of professional judgment and responsibility.

In 1967, at the time of the South Vietnamese presidential elections, the Johnson Administration sponsored a full-fledged pseudo-event on a par with the Honolulu conference. In response to published and broadcast doubts about the validity and fairness of those elections, it sent a handpicked team of "observers," headed by a loyal party Democrat, Governor Richard Hughes, of New Jersey, to witness the balloting. None of the group spoke or understood Vietnamese, and none of them had any but the most superficial background in Vietnamese politics, nor did they as a group care. They had been sent not so much for the purpose of observation as to bestow a benediction. The group predictably found everything perfectly kosher, though a wide range of undemocratic practices on the part of the Thieu-Ky military regime, from bribery and intimidation to blocking press coverage of their opponents, had been documented by seasoned Vietnam reporters. Nor did their enthusiasm noticeably wane when they were told that at a number of rallies they attended the secret police had interrogated members of the audience who had the temerity to ask critical questions of pro-

Thieu/Ky speakers and candidates. Some U.S. newspapers ran critical press reports of the election campaign, but most gave equal—and many gave greater—space and prominence to the highly suspect and, to say the least, thoroughly unqualified views of the "observers."

To allow the President and his Administration such control of the image he projects to the nation is an obvious and dangerous abdication of independence and responsibility on the part of the press. Why is this permitted? With television, most commentators agree, it is largely due to a sensitivity to the power of the President and the executive branch and to a concern for the effect that particular power can have on corporate profits. But perhaps an equally important factor is the tendency of the press to pander to the "cult of personality" surrounding the President and the bureaucratic extensions of his power. The tendency is particularly tempting to television's show-biz values, although broadcast executives and journalists defend themselves against the charge of superficiality by contending that since they operate in the dimension of time (as opposed to space for newspapers), broadcast news must necessarily be a headline service. At the same time we are all familiar with the common practice of devoting significant segments of that valuable time to the President's golf game or the welfare of his pet beagles.*

A mutate of the pseudoevent, growing out of the same manipulative soil, is receiving increasing attention from newsmen and critics of broadcasting concerned with the state of their trade. This is what MacNeil calls "campaigning by commercial." This monstrosity, born of a union between political and commercial hucksterism in the bordello of Madison Avenue, may well be the scale model of the perfect Snow Machine. Once envisioned by many as a powerful new means for enhancing the democratic process, a platform permitting the electorate to compare the candidates' persons and their views on issues, a place of debate and genuine contest, television has become the principal instrument for eroding the democratic

---

* Again we have an example of a highly successful attempt to move the center of argument rightward. Newsmen who might formerly (in the case of television) have been arguing this issue among themselves now find themselves on the defensive for having merely analyzed and commented upon a Presidential television appearance in its immediate aftermath.

electoral process and separating political campaigning from reality. The Kennedy-Nixon debates, the first of their kind since the Lincoln-Douglas confrontation, were most likely also the last of their kind. Instead we are increasingly given candidates and issues shaped, groomed, edited, and packaged with the same kind of half-truths, distortions, lies, and lacunae which promote a brand of cigarettes as the answer to one's social and sexual problems. In 1968 Richard Nixon, committed to a low-risk front-runner's campaign, devoted most of his campaign expenditures to the production of slick, expertly done political commercials for network television. In fact, he may be considered by historians to have been the first television commercial to win the Presidency. And we may see the day when Presidential elections become simply a contest between the two most successful advertising agencies in the country (both controlled, perhaps, by the same industrial conglomerate).

There is another phenomenon similar to the pseudoevent but different both as to source and substance: the demonstration. A demonstration is a pseudoevent insofar as it is a contrived happening whose main purpose is the acquisition of space or time on the platform of the news media from which the thoughts, complaints, and demands of its organizers and participants can be addressed to the general public. Most demonstrations, however, are a mixture of the pseudo and the real; and many of them begin as pseudoevents only to become very real events indeed—such as Chicago.

A number of civil-rights leaders have become expert technicians in the trade. One of the best is Andrew Young, an official of the Southern Christian Leadership Conference and one of the late Martin Luther King's most talented lieutenants. The civil-rights demonstrations in Selma, Alabama, in the spring of 1965 were a classic and successful example of the genre. Their purpose was to secure voting registration for black people and the federal assistance obviously necessary to that end. Their means was a dramatic gesture, a march from Selma to Montgomery which would predictably bring on a confrontation with the white power structure and draw the focus of the national news media on their plight, generate national pressure for governmental action, and so forth. For a week the demonstrators were prevented from marching, and their activities were confined to an area no larger than three square blocks. But each day, under the leadership of Andy Young, they demonstrated where they were (and where the television cameras by now were, too). And each day they added something new to hold the attention of the fickle press: a confrontation with the police lines blocking them, attempts by groups of youngsters to break out of the area in which they were confined and run downtown, a marathon vigil in the street after the beating and death of a white clergyman from their group—most of these carefully timed to insure that television coverage made the evening news.

This kind of semi-pseudoevent differs from the real thing also in its source, the reasons for it. The manipulation of the press by the President stems from its ready availability to him, from the habit of nearly unlimited access to the media. The civil-rights demonstrations developed as a response to a situation in which great numbers of Americans with problems and grievances had almost no access to the media, a situation in which the more glaring and widespread injustices were not being communicated, certainly not communicated effectively. In many respects mass, organized demonstrations are necessary responses of ordinary people to the massing of economic and political power elsewhere—in the great corporations and conglomerates and in government—and the growing awareness among Americans that free speech can be a frustrating exercise unless that speech can somehow be made effective as well as free.

We are dealing here with a new form of communication developed to keep pace with a society and an age which technically facilitate manipulation and control of opinion. With revolutionary communicative technology increasingly centralized and increasingly devoted to commercial and political conditioning and diverted from communication, those elements of our population which do not share in, and whose interests are not advanced by, that centralization must find an effective form of communication or suffer in silence. We have been for some time in the throes of major social realignments, and that process today is even more accelerated. We see emerging around us new forces, new issues, new power relationships, and new institutions and practices which reflect those relationships. As made evident by the Kerner Report, the press, which should take the lead (or at least be somewhere near the front) in adjusting to them, coping with them, and understanding their implications, has failed to really come to grips with these forces—in large part, perhaps, because it has failed to understand and cope with the effects and implications of its own changing technology. We seem to be drifting into what might be called 'Pavlovian democracy, with much of our eyes and ears—the press— not only unaware of the development but unaware of its own suicidal role in it. This failure of the press, reflected by ignorance and, in many cases, attempts to mask that ignorance by hiding behind the statements, attitudes, and assumptions of Establishment officials and functionaries, has done much to breed further mistrust of itself among minority groups and to intensify an already serious social and political polarization.

CHAPTER 10 ■

The Nascent Profession

"Explain yourself!"
"I can't explain myself, I'm afraid, sir," said Alice, "because I'm not myself, you see."
—Lewis Carroll, *Alice in Wonderland*

American journalism has come a long way from the days of Ben Franklin and Philip Freneau, when American newspapers and magazines were little more than vehicles for the personal opinions of their publishers or the indentured organs of political parties. In the last fifty years particularly, American journalism has begun to develop some of the discipline, the collective self-respect and awareness of a special mission or function, and the general standards of competence and ethics which characterize a profession. But the key word here is *begun*. Although almost all working journalists think of themselves as professionals—and although some of them genuinely are—the press in general, both individuals and organizations, possesses the basic qualities of a profession only sporadically and unevenly at best. And whatever its absolute gains over the years, the press has lost ground relative to the heavy responsibilities placed upon it by a complex, technologized, and rapidly changing society. At this juncture it would seem critical that the press adopt those professional characteristics if it is to adequately perform its function of informing, enlightening, and educating, if it is to do its part in leading a confused and fearful people away from the brink of disaster, if it is to reestablish its own credibility with the American people and present an effective front against the trends and forces challenging it and democracy itself today. That this is possible is not at all certain. But it is clear that it is necessary.

In *Responsibility in Mass Communication* William L. Rivers and Wilbur Schramm discuss the need for the "professionalization" of the press, first observing that journalism cannot fully be a profession in the traditional sense that medicine and law are professions. Its practitioners are not, as a rule, self-employed and therefore independently responsible for the ultimate quality of their service; they are employees of larger organizations. They do not operate within a discrete, specialized, and highly developed and codified body of knowledge on which examinations might be given and licenses issued; their subject matter, instead, covers the full spectrum of human activities. Also, the practice of licensing journalists and disciplining those so licensed for incompetence or malpractice would be an obvious and highly dangerous erosion of the First Amendment and a powerful tool for press control. Rivers and Schramm add, however:

> Having made all these technical points, let us argue that we can expect professional standards, attitudes, and behavior from mass communication. And let us suggest that a profession develops, not by asking how another profession is organized, but by asking what kind of behavior is necessary to public-service obligations. If that question is seriously asked, thoughtfully answered and acted upon, communication will be on the road to professional status.

But the difficulties in professionalizing the press involve more than just its unique and necessarily amorphous nature. Control of the journalist by the business manager and the imposition of the values of sales charts, ratings, and circulation figures on the business of gathering, reporting, and interpreting the news is not a situation easily altered by the working journalist with the best will in the world.

A serious initial problem is that the press lacks adequate

machinery even for self-evaluation. The intellectual foundation and "bureau of standards" for most professions are the professional schools. But with only a few exceptions (notable among them, Columbia University and the University of Missouri), the journalism departments in American colleges are the poor stepchildren of the academic family and considered, with some justice, along with speech departments as a refuge for the slow and less qualified—an academic welfare plan for those poor in talent—and that is often as true of faculty as it is of students. Further, there is no really comprehensive or effective *professional* organization in American journalism. What organizations do exist divide themselves along the lines of labor and management, both categories concerning themselves with little more than the economic interests of their members. It may be argued that the same can be said of the American Medical Association. I would offer no argument there, except to paraphrase Rivers and Schramm and observe that a profession does not develop by observing the corruption of another profession.

Given the economic structure of the American press, there is, of course, no alternative to trade-union activities and organization on the part of the journalist. Journalism will never truly become a profession, however, as long as the interests and techniques of trade unionism are allowed to override the most fundamental professional values. The problem is especially acute in television, since TV newsmen do not even have their own union but are organized by the American Federation of Television and Radio Artists, another practice that tends to fuzz the line between news and entertainment. (It is a situation that caused NBC's Chet Huntley to rebel during the AFTRA strike of 1967 and cross the picket line, refusing to acknowledge the authority of a performers' union over newsmen.) As Robert MacNeil has observed, the practice of rewarding newsmen in the same manner that actors are paid—that is, on a fee over base salary arrangement for each item used on a sponsored news broadcast—powerfully whets the reporter's appetite for the easy and quickly done story and decreases his interest in digging below the surface of events or covering a story that takes more than a few minutes to film.

But much more than the removal of such negative influence is needed. The development of the profession requires positive organization along professional lines and with professional performance and the advancement of professional standards as the primary consideration. A union whose shop meetings included discussion of the professional quality of a station's or network's news operation, local meetings concerned with the coverage of a city's issues and problems, conventions devoted to the same concerns on a national scale, and bargaining practices that would integrate the protection of the members' economic welfare and job conditions with the advancement of professional quality would do much to complete the birth of American journalism as a bona-fide profession. But this is still only the beginning of a necessary process. Given the freedom to professionalize, the press would still be faced with the need to redefine, in a most fundamental way, its function in contemporary society as well as values and practices that have long seemed elementary and axiomatic.

The News and Its Values

What is news? That is a question whose answer is not uniformly agreed to even in the trade. On its answer, however, rest both the nature and the quality of journalism. "News is the unusual and the unexpected," NBC's David Brinkley once stated. "If an airplane departs on time, arrives on time, it isn't news," he explained. "If it crashes, regrettably, it is."* The definition was an ad-lib response to a criticism of the alleged tendency of the press to focus on unrepresentative but dramatic militants and trouble-makers, what some call the sensationalist negativism of the electronic press. David Brinkley is too intelligent a professional to offer or even consider his answer a sufficient definition. But it is an important part of any definition of the news, and it describes what the news very often is. The question remains whether or not this is what the news should be.

If a cross section of reporters, editors, and news directors were polled on the same question, the answers would probably be variations on three themes: (1) that which has importance for the public

* "The Whole World Is Watching," P.B.L.

business, (2) that which is new (and unusual or unexpected), (3) that which sells papers or boosts ratings. All three criteria are used by almost any news organization in selecting what is to be printed or broadcast and what prominence it is to be given. Where news organizations vary, from one another as well as from the ideal, is in the relative weight afforded each criterion in the decision process. Whereas, theoretically, most reporters and editors would agree that the order of priority should be as listed above, in practice most news organizations operate from the bottom up, with maximum profit the arbiter of all other considerations. It is one of the profound weaknesses of "free enterprise" society that disparate and critical social functions have, as *the* criterion of success, a goal essentially unrelated to and often in contradiction of the functions themselves. This has been notoriously true of both medicine and law, and it is one instance in which the press fully meets the standards set by its more codified sister professions.

If the basic function of the press in a democratic society is to provide the people with the information necessary to the conduct of government and the general public business, to apprise them of events and trends at home and abroad relevant to that business, then *news* must be defined and evaluated in the context of that function. But what is important to the public business? And what is most important? One does not question Brinkley's assertion that an airplane crash is news but a routinely successful flight is not. What one must question, however, is that the news of the airplane crash is frequently given greater prominence than public hearings on utility rates, Senate deliberations over a new tax bill, or hearings of the Foreign Relations Committee on a treaty or a foreign-aid package. A man goes berserk and murders his wife and children. In all but a few papers around the country the story will headline the next edition, yet an important school bond issue or a story on the failures and inequities in a welfare program will get space deep on an inside page, if they make the edition at all. Although tragic and dramatic, both the crash and the miltiple murder are accidents; they are essentially meaningless events that tell the reader or viewer nothing useful to him personally or as a responsible citizen of a democracy and little about his society or the world he lives in that he does not already know. Unless they are somehow meaningful in a larger context (e.g., the crash exposes faulty airplane construction or poor air-traffic control), such stories belong on or close to the obituary page. Properly, the crash should be back-paged and any subsequent finding that construction, training, or flight procedures were inadequate should be front-paged and headlined. Unfortunately, the general practice is quite the reverse. Indeed, to continue with this particular example, crash investigations are rarely made public in any meaningful detail, nor are the relevant statistics from air disasters publicly collated. In what circumstances do a greater or lesser number of passengers survive a crash? Which type of aircraft are involved in the largest and the smallest number of crashes? Which airlines have the best and the poorest records? What are the major causes of crashes? These are matters important to the public business and of considerable personal interest to anyone who flies, even occasionally. But they are seldom dealt with in the press, even in the aftermath of major air disasters, and they are almost never dealt with prominently.

Both the airplane crash and the murderous lunatic receive coverage in the press in proportion to their shock value but out of all proportion to their relevance to the public interest. This is generally true of disasters and crime news, but worse, such coverage is often limited to those aspects of the story providing immediate shock value, whereas a welfare story or a story on the general climate of the local ghetto is run obscurely. Until, of course, a riot occurs. When that happens, we are greeted in our newspapers and on our television screens with the news of violence and bloodshed first and then with the draconian warnings of public officials and the rantings of the law-and-order addicts; we have been brought face to face with a situation whose roots stretch deep into years of misery and deprivation, and when it is over, we understand it only as an explosion resulting from bad habits and bad elements. In short, we do not understand it, have learned nothing, and may even have lost what understanding we might have had. And the press has failed dismally in its cardinal responsibility. The institution whose task is to help us understand the world around us and the true nature and scope of the problems we face has, instead, pandered to our ignorances and prejudices, flattered our lack of attention and concern, and profited on our simple-minded views of man and society.

There are those in the business who argue that the press has no business arrogating to itself the determination of what is important for the public to read in newspapers or see on home screens. Like their counterparts in the entertainment industry who insist that the public gets what it wants, they ignore the fact that mass communication is a two-way street in at least one respect: Public response may determine what editors and news directors provide, but the converse is also true, for the response is conditioned and an expectation is created by what the public is provided. As mentioned before, a number of critics of current press practices have contended, quite rightly, that lack of public interest in many important local and national issues (as opposed to murders, airplane crashes, riots, and the sexual habits of public figures) is to be ascribed to the failure of the press to make the relevance and importance of those issues manifest. Deciding what is important or most important is to be clearly differentiated from Richard M. Harnett's warning about the dangers of news directors and executives deciding what is good or bad for people to know. It is the difference between full, intelligent disclosure and partial disclosure, or "restraint." Harnett argues that the latter is not only no antidote for the poison of sensationalism but is likely to be more lethal than the poison it seeks to counter.

Television news directors and producers are constantly concerned with the problem of holding their audiences, of maintaining the viewers' interest. That would be fine if they were equally concerned with their responsibility as journalists for interesting those viewers in issues of true importance. Unfortunately, in any conflict the latter inevitably falls victim to the former. As a result, although a news program may hold the interest of its audience, it is frequently a feat of consummate unimportance except to the station or network and its sponsors. The press fails its mandate in this manner, and it also becomes an active part of that manipulative process which it fights in its dealings with government and which is anathema to its cause and death to its function. The effort to create interest is legitimate and honest communication and a prime responsibility of a free press. But to structure the news on the basis of preexisting interests for the sake of holding an audience or maintaining or increasing ratings and circulation figures is basic manipulation: The news, the profession of journalism, is simply being exploited for the purpose of delivering an audience to sponsors and advertisers for commercial propagandizing.

There is one widely voiced criticism regarding the problem of negativism in the news which should be countered: the charge that the press deals only or inordinately with the dark side of things, that it emphasizes the negative and ignores the positive. In such criticism the word "sensational" is used as if it were synonymous with "negative." But these are two very different terms. Sensationalism is really a form of pandering, playing on fear, prejudice, and morbidity. The negative, however, is irreducibly the basic stuff of legitimate journalism, and it is here that Brinkley's narrow definition of news is perfectly valid. "Why don't you say something good about the country?" and "Why don't you show the positive side of things?" are familiar plaints to most newsmen. Those who make such requests, however, do not want journalism, they want chamber of commerce propaganda; they do not want to be informed, they want to be flattered and patted on the back. Their demands are simply one more way of saying, "Why don't you get on the team?" Journalism must be largely negative for the simple reason that the journalist, like the doctor, deals in pathology. And who would think of asking his doctor to concentrate on what is right with him? By the same token—by the criterion of importance to the public business—hunger, oppression, riots, wars, and the conditions that breed them are properly news, whereas peace and healthy people are not. Corruption in city hall is news, whereas an ordinary, honest public servant competently doing what he is paid for is not. Dangerously poor construction of a housing project is a matter that demands public attention and remedial action; a competently built structure is not. This is not to say that accounts of progress, positive and constructive programs, and stories of achievement, dedication, and purpose do not have a place in the news—far from it. It *is* to say that such matters are of considerably less importance and carry a much lower priority than persistent and emergent problems that the public must understand and attempt to solve. Indeed, a more cogent criticism to be made of the press is that its negativism is neither wide nor deep enough, that its exploration of problems and issues tends to be too superficial and erratic, and that it wastes far too much space and time on positive frills at the expense of negative substance.

The booster mentality is already far too evident in American journalism, as was evidenced by the behavior of the Chicago press before the 1968 Democratic convention—and after it, when the city's newspapers had gotten over the shock of having their own reporters kicked arround. Prior to the convention the Chicago *Sun-Times* had not only ordered its reporters to play down coverage of the peace march of April 27 (during which police used their clubs to dispel the marchers) but had buried it at the bottom of a story on a V.F.W. Loyalty Day parade, a poorly attended and altogether insignificant event. Later, as the week of the convention approached, the Chicago press exhibited similar civic protectionism and paranoia at the prospect of a mass influx of out-of-town demonstrators. During the week of general mayhem some angry words were printed in Chicago about the mayor and his police, but the city's press by and large later recovered itself and decided it had overreacted. That was journalistic boosterism with a vengeance! Nor are such attitudes and practices confined to Chicago. Editorial decisions based on civic loyalty and parochial pride are common vices of the local press and are responsible for much repression, distortion, and general news management.

Any serious discussion of news values and priorities must also deal with the inordinately reactive nature of much contemporary journalism, its overreliance on the statements and activities of public figures and "experts." If there is hunger in America, what is the core of the story, the fact of that hunger or the "fact-finding" tour of a congressional committee to "study" it? If the answer seems obviously the first, the general practice is clearly the second. What did the average newspaper-reader or television-viewer know about the plight of the Eskimo before Senator Edward Kennedy's controversial Alaskan trip in the spring of 1969? Indeed, what has

he heard of it since? Occasionally, the activities of a reporter or a
news organization will spark action from public officials. Unfortunately, the reverse is more often the case. One sometimes gets the
impression nothing is so until and unless a sufficiently prominent
personage says it is. The record of press initiative in the area of
independent investigative reporting is a poor one. There is, for
instance, an obviously and immensely rich field for investigative
reporting in the nation's capital—in the various agencies and
departments of the federal government. But it is a potential poorly
tapped, even by such deservedly prestigious national publications as
The New York Times. The result of the tendency of the press to act
as a transmission belt for the opinions, attitudes, and priorities of
public figures and agencies instead of digging out its own facts and
ordering its own priorities is the progressive loss of its independence
and a heightened vulnerability to manipulation. And it offers a
powerful argument for those who view the press as nothing more
than an arm of the Establishment.

With respect to coverage of government operations, the source of
the problem is not so much laziness or incompetence on the part of
reporters but rather an information process established by the
manipulative tendencies of government officials and agencies. This
process is protected by an unconstrained competition among the
press which prevents effective professional cooperation even for the
purposes of maintaining basic ethical standards and professional
self-defense. Earlier I referred to the dangers of governmental
information practices and the tendency to utilize the press as
"handmaidens." A proper share of the blame belongs to the press,
however, for it must be said that the ability of government bureaucracies to so use reporters is more often a matter of seduction than
of rape.

During the latter days of the 1968 Tet offensive the U.S. press
czar in Saigon, Barry Zorthian, invited reporters to his office on the
third floor of the JUSPAO building following the regular five
o'clock press briefing. Zorthian held such "backgrounders" at frequent intervals for the few reporters who cared to come along and
chat and catch up on the thinking of American officialdom in
Saigon. This session, however, was a combination of "deep back-

ground" and "off-the-record." These terms are jargon for the kind of attribution a reporter is allowed to give information supplied him by officials, and they also determine whether or not the information can be used at all. At most formal press briefings reporters are told they can identify the source by name or that they can ascribe the information to "a spokesman." In either case the information is officially and publicly vouched for. If a briefing is labeled "background," it is not to be identified in any way as an official statement, though the reporter may use the information as "the feeling in official circles here is . . ." or variations thereof. "Deep background" means that the information is in no way to be ascribed, even inferentially. If it is used, it is the reporter's responsibility, and he must use it as if it were his own discovery or his own opinion. If the discussion is placed "off-the-record," he cannot use the information at all. The penalties for ignoring these limitations are (1) the drying up of the source, if it involves a personal or individual contact, or (2) the ostracism of the offender by officials and sometimes by his own colleagues: Both are serious professional liabilities. Actually, the system has a legitimate and useful purpose. It enables officials to discuss sensitive matters with reporters in varying degrees of confidence without committing themselves, their agencies, or the United States to a position before that position is taken. Ideally, it means that the reporter can acquire much greater insight and information than would be possible if officials felt he was nothing but a microphone transmitting to the world at large. But little in this world is ideal, and the abuse of the system by government officials has, with the acquiescence of the press, turned it into a major tool for manipulating the press.

The session with Zorthian on this day was held to discuss the general results of the offensive, the evaluation of which was just beginning. The meeting had been underway less than five minutes when one of the assembled reporters got up in a rage, denounced Zorthian, announced that he was not going to be a party to off-the-record confidences, and strode angrily out of the room. His colleagues were temporarily speechless, and although a few made snide and disparaging remarks about him later, many were clearly abashed. Why did he do it? He was not only an experienced journal-

ist, but he was also the Washington bureau chief of a major metropolitan daily, the Boston *Globe;* he was not a rash young man who
had yet to learn the ropes of his trade. He did it because, on the contrary, he knew enough to recognize the trap. Zorthian's "deep background" information was, to say the least, highly questionable
conjecture. But far worse, his "off-the-record" contributions included a great deal already known or likely to be independently
surmised.

When a reporter remains at a briefing or allows a conversation to
continue in his presence after the words "off-the-record" have been
uttered, he has committed himself to observe a confidence. If he
acquires the same information independently after the confidence
session is over, he will still, in most cases, consider himself bound to
silence for the simple reason that his off-the-record source is unlikely to believe in the independence of his second source. Knowing
this, officials not infrequently move to dam up speculation and
conjecture too close to an embarrassing or delicate truth; sometimes they even block the publishing of easily obtained fact by
preemption: They reveal it *off-the-record*. The practice flourishes in
Washington as well as elsewhere, but, as with many aspects of
bureaucratic pathology, nowhere so feverishly as in Vietnam.

A more commonly used and consequently more important variation of the confidence game has quite another, nearly opposite,
purpose. That is the "deep background" confidence and its in-
genious mutation, the "leak." Both are methods employed to get
the reporter to say what the bureaucrat wants said but doesn't want
to be heard saying. The real bonus is that the resulting story comes
out in many cases as the reporter's independent finding or his
considered opinion—in any case free of the taint of official line or
official self-interest. This is at least partially accomplished even
when the reporter uses "identifying" circumlocutions such as "informed sources," "reliable sources," or the like. The planting of
stories, ideas, information and misinformation, as well as the float-
ing of trial balloons, is most often done in this manner. The
practice is so widespread and frequent that newsmen regularly
assigned to government agencies such as the Pentagon literally
become mouthpieces for the organizations they are assigned to

cover. In this respect the situation is far worse in Washington than in Saigon or anywhere else American reporters work with American officials. In Vietnam most reporters cover the entire spectrum of U.S. and South Vietnamese activities. A comparable beat in Washington would be one that ranged across the entire spectrum of government activities, from the federal agencies to the committees of Congress to the Supreme Court. Such assignments, however, are rare in Washington. Most news of the Pentagon, for example, comes from reporters regularly assigned, day in and day out, to that institution. For this reason the Washington press corps, although comprising some of the best talent in American journalism, is probably the most corrupted and manipulated group of newsmen in American journalism.

Why do newsmen permit such egregious abuse of their function? There are a number of answers that add up to the fact that they have little choice, and the reason lies in a professional competition unchecked by effective concern for ethical standards or common professional interest. Why was the Boston *Globe* man the only one to walk out of Zorthian's press conference? Because those who might have wanted to could not afford to. The *Globe* reporter was in Saigon on a brief junket of two weeks. He was competing with no one, Barry Zorthian's sessions were of no particular importance to him, and he could afford to act on principle (he would be filled in on all of it later anyway, and he could then, with clear conscience in both directions, go ahead and use the information as he saw fit, full identification and all). This is meant in no way to denigrate his action but only to indicate that he was far freer than his colleagues. They *were* in competition, Vietnam was their daily, weekly, monthly beat, and Zorthian's tête-à-têtes were important to them for insight, guidance as to official thinking, and so on, even though they sometimes paid a professional price for it. In any event no single one or group of them could afford to be left out as long as any of their competition remained in. The same kind of pressure sometimes forces reporters to file stories generated by a deep backgrounder or a leak which they don't really believe. The information is equally available to the competition, this is the only way it can be used, *ergo*. . . . Psychic defenses and occupational interests combine to produce true believers and relatively sincere mouthpieces.

The defense against this kind of prostitution remains largely theoretical. Many reporters, particularly the young ones who have yet to be sufficiently brainwashed or hardened into cynics (a combination of the two is common), ask themselves and each other, "Why don't we refuse to cooperate? Why don't we all leave this confidential little session, go back to our offices, and write up the whole goddamned thing for what it is?" Their own answer is that they can't, because the newspapers, magazines, broadcasting stations, and networks they work for aren't interested. Competitive access to government sources is more important than the quality of information acquired or the integrity of their public service. A similar pattern is to be found in the press coverage of many state capitals and city halls. The individual reporter, even if he finds that a majority of his colleagues share his distaste for the situation, has little choice but to go along or get out. Reporters may be unionized, but they are not professionally organized. They cannot act in concert because they have no organization interested in such action. They cannot act professionally because they are not yet, not sufficiently, a profession.

Objectivity and Truth

If there is a single dominant shibboleth in contemporary journalism, it is "objectivity." In tandem with full disclosure, its canons occupy a place in the presumed hierarchy of journalistic ethics comparable to medicine's Hippocratic oath. Unfortunately, it is a principle observed most often in the breach or to avoid the perils of seeking the truth, and it is often prostituted as an excuse for superficiality or as a cover for the less than true.

Formal objectivity is a concept often used with very nonobjective selectivity. In the case of ghetto unrest, news organizations of a conservative bent frequently confine their coverage to the hard, verifiable, or documented facts of the event itself because they feel that to go deeper into such an issue, to search out the background of unrest and provide a larger context in which it may be understood (interpretation), would be to argue extenuation of an act they see simply as a crime, an affront to law and the traditional order of things, and thereby to invite sympathy if not approval. On the other hand, the fact that objectively verifiable reality is often partisan, that it frequently supports one side of an argument against another, is one of the major problems of "balance," which is considered a corollary virtue to objectivity. The weighing of various points of view against one another and against the facts is an integral aspect of sound reporting. But the common practice of confusing balance with objectivity, and vice versa, defeats the basic purpose of both. Having reported two sides of a debate does not relieve the journalist or his organization of the responsibility for determining the winner with respect to the available knowledge, nor does it relieve him from attempting to determine the objective truth of the issue apart from the debaters' arguments, however that might upset the "balance." Balance is often used as a substitute for objective reporting, just as superficial objectivity is frequently a substitute for full and detailed inquiry. Broadcasting is particularly prone to this vice, being largely more concerned with "fairness" than with truth, and with the illusion of professionalism than with its substance.

Strict insistence on the forms (i.e., appearance) of objectivity often defeats the purpose of the discipline, which is to provide the public with coherent factual information. For instance, the work of the reporter, limited in theory to the objective representation of developments, is passed on to the reading public as though it were not filtered through a human consciousness, when in fact it is so filtered; the presence of a byline (still largely eschewed by the wire services) does little to mitigate the deception. Such filtering is, of course, not only unavoidable but absolutely necessary in reporting the news. The hard facts of developing events often have little meaning for the average reader or viewer until arranged in some context—related, interpreted if you will—by the reporter filing the story. But the process should be clear to the reader, and often it is not clear at all. Thus, in the highly professional *New York Times* one is presented with the opinions and analyses of "observers" without ever being told that the term most often stands for the journalist and his reporter colleagues. The writer's editors and other journalists recognize the code, but the public does not. Thus the opinions of an unknown number of reporters can be misrepresented as the consensus of informed opinion on the scene. Maintaining the fiction of the reporter as an eye without an I is not in the best interests of sound journalism. All too frequently, the inability of a reporter to detail the facts and then explain what they mean leads him to edit and arrange them in a manner that projects his interpretation as inescapable conclusion instead of informed opinion.

■ CHAPTER 11 ■

The Mission of the Press

*Americans have been given to a kind of historical amnesia
that masks much of their turbulent past. Probably all nations
share this tendency to sweeten memories of their past through
collective repression, but Americans have probably magnified
this process of selective recollection, owing to our historic
vision of ourselves as a latter-day chosen people, a new Jerusalem.*
    —from *Violence in America: Historical and Comparative
    Perspectives*, a report made to the National Commission
    on the Causes and Prevention of Violence, edited by
    Hugh Davis Graham and Ted Robert Gurr

*amnesia [Gr., = forgetfulness], condition characterized by loss
of memory for long or short intervals of time. It may be caused
by shock, injury, senility, severe illness, or mental disease. In
some cases, memory of events prior to the illness is lost; in others,
events following the illness are forgotten. One form of the
condition known as tropic amnesia or coast memory affects
white men on the west coast of Africa; this condition is thought
to be hysteric in origin. . . . To cure amnesia, attempts are
made to establish associations with the past by suggestion.*
    —*The Columbia Encyclopedia*

George Santayana's dictum that those who forget history are con-
demned to relive it may be one of the most overworked clichés of
our age, but like many clichés it has a certain validity. It is no ex-

aggeration to suggest that those who do not remember who and
where they have been will be hard put to identify who they are
and determine where they are going. And at no time in their history
have Americans been so confused about their identity, location, and
direction as they are at present. To put it a different way, the habit
of memory repression referred to in the Graham-Gurr report quoted
above has a tendency to spread from memory of the past to perception of the present. Those unaware of the violence in America's
past are often equally innocent concerning the violence in her soul:
social injustice, economic exploitation, and civil decay. Brought
face to face with demonstrations, riots, and rising crime rates, they
perceive those symptoms—with the same primitive conceptual
tools that have always served man in moments of confusion, ignorance, and fear—as the work of evil forces or the inevitable
retribution for broken taboos.

The American history taught in America's high schools (and in
many college courses as well) could be more aptly labeled American mythology. Heavy on dates, treaties, and acts of Congress, it is
very light on reality, for it is taught more in the spirit of that
peculiarly American phenomenon called boosterism than out of a
desire to reveal the past as it truly was. This new Jerusalem was
built as much by greed and fear, oppression and exploitation,
Indian blood and black slavery, as by any of the litany of virtues we
sing in self-congratulation. In a nation that proclaimed all men to
be created equal, slavery was abolished only after a fratricidal war,
and then only technically. This land of great wealth and political
progressivism has been the scene of industrial exploitation and
misery as great as that of any European country; it "has had the
bloodiest and most violent labor history of any industrial nation in
the world."* We are a nation that avoided the ultimate violence of
revolution largely because of the geographical safety-valve provided by the West, where urban misery and exploitation could be
traded for danger and adventure, where industrial frustrations

* Philip Taft and Philip Ross, "American Labor Violence: Its Causes, Character and Outcome," Chapter 8 in *The History of Violence in America: A Report
to the National Commission on the Causes and Prevention of Violence,* edited
by Hugh Davis Graham and Ted Robert Gurr (New York: Bantam Books, Inc.,
1969), p. 281.

could be vented on the primitive Indian, and where a life of poverty could be transformed by those with sufficient courage and stamina by plundering the Indian (and the Mexican) of his lands. Such is the heritage of America, or at least a significant part of it. It is not a picture that comports well with our public view of ourselves and our history, but it is one that is vital to national self-knowledge.

Reporters covering civil-rights activities in the South during the first few years of the 1960's became accustomed to hearing the most pathetic expressions of historical amnesia from white southerners who patiently explained that, except for some malcontents and "outside agitators," the black man in the South was happy and satisfied. *Their* "Nigras" wanted nothing to do with the civil-rights movement. As proof of this assertion they would inevitably quote conversations with maids or cooks or other black employees to that effect. The white employer, for the most part, remained unaware that a portion of the meagre wages he paid that same servant frequently went to the Southern Christian Leadership Conference or the Congress of Racial Equality or the N.A.A.C.P. to finance the movement's activities in the local area. The white southerner who made such claims, however, generally believed them himself; it was more than hypocrisy or propaganda, it was ignorance of the true relationship between himself and the black man, ignorance of the effect that four hundred years of slavery and post-slavery subjugation, repression, and exploitation had had both on the black man and on himself. The most profound kind of "coast memory" permitted him to visualize the old South as the setting for Stephen Foster's songs, the Civil War as the heroic struggle for southern freedom and independence from the Yankee North, and the present (in terms of race relations) as just fine if not the best of all possible worlds. He had never understood his past and, consequently, had no conceptual tools with which to perceive the reality of the present. And how shocked were the good white people of Birmingham and Jackson and Savannah and Selma when masses of black demonstrators coursed through their streets and sat-in at their lunch counters and boycotted their buses. A similar and probably equal shock was felt later when riots that were almost insurrections swept nonsouthern cities from Los Angeles to New York, where the impairment of historical memory and present perception similarly nourished one another.

The institution that bears responsibility along with the educational system for public awareness and understanding of public problems is, of course, the mass media, and especially that portion of the media we characterize as the press. American journalism must therefore accept partial responsibility for what Graham and Gurr have chosen to call "historical amnesia" in the United States, and even greater responsibility for its continuing impact on present perception.

In his book, *The Making of a Quagmire,* David Halberstam described the terrible experience of witnessing the fiery self-immolation of Tich Quang Duc, the Buddhist monk whose death on a Saigon street in 1963 galvanized the forces that toppled the Diem regime. Recalling his own reaction to the grisly scene, the reporter wrote: "I had never felt such conflicting emotions: one part of me wanted to extinguish the fire, another warned that I had no right to interfere, another told me that it was too late, another asked whether I was a reporter or a human being."

Most reporters with much experience and any degree of sensitivity have had occasion to ask themselves Halberstam's question, and many people from all walks of life have asked similar questions about reporters: "How can they be detached at a time like this?" "How can they simply *observe,* scribble notes, and snap pictures at such a time?" There is no easy answer to such a question; indeed, at times it seems as though it is not possible to be a reporter and a human being at the same time. The reporter must observe with as much detachment as he can muster in order simply to report a scene or event with accuracy and clarity. But the human being must respond to human situations, if only emotionally; he must, at times, take sides, if only in his own mind. It can, of course, be said that it is not necessary for an honest, competent journalist, dedicated to the discovery of the truth, to wear the chastity belt of strict neutrality. After all, the truth, whatever else it might be, is seldom neutral. But that answer does not solve the problem posed by the question. The question really asks whether the importance of the reporter's function is great enough to require, and therefore excuse, behavior different from that expected of other men.

The question is not seriously posed for the doctor, whose emotional detachment and objective approach to human suffering is generally considered a necessary aspect of a critical function. Nor is it asked, at least to the same degree, of the lawyer, who must frequently assert and defend the innocence of a man whom he knows to be guilty and whom both he and the public at large may despise. The difference is that both doctor and lawyer share with the public a sense of their own special and necessary mission. It is generally agreed that in any relevant situation their function is the maximum service they can provide and that it is of critical importance to society. That sense of mission is the moral foundation of any profession; it defines the professional role, dictates its ethical canons, and protects the function against the encroachments of conflicting demands. The Hippocratic oath requires the doctor to be a doctor before he is a Protestant, Republican, New Yorker, or even an American. Unfortunately, journalism has no Hippocratic oath, and what sense of mission it has developed over the years is undernourished, thinly and unevenly spread, and frequently rejected. Many journalists, perhaps most, consider themselves national patriots, regional propagandists and municipal boosters, liberals or conservatives, before they consider themselves practitioners of a profession with duties that take precedence over these commitments. And if the journalist himself has little conviction of mission and little concern for its integrity, it should not be too surprising if the general public lacks awareness of it. Journalism today is still a trade in the service of the wrong clients, turning out a product that many find of questionable utility.

Index

Index